MW01244121

Chris's book is a boots-on-the-ground primer for anyone in sales. It is completely from his heart and written in a plain-speaking style you will enjoy. You'll get the advantage of Chris's successful sales approach broken down and easily understood and implemented. Chris is the real deal, and so is his book.

Frank Somma, Sales Expert, Professional
Speaker and Coach, New Jersey

Chris-Michael is a tenured and talented sales professional who exemplifies the energy, enthusiasm, and hustle of a highly effective seller. His experiences and successes should be considered best practices for those looking to improve their sales prowess.

Jennifer Staub, Vice President of Sales Training,
Nexstar Media Group, Harrisburg, PA

Had the opportunity to read *Life of a Salesperson* by Chris-Michael Carangelo. It was a great read that lays out a streamlined approach to the insurance marketing process that is a must read for all producers. If you want to become a trusted advisor, just as your clients view their Attorneys and CPAs, pick this up today.

Joe Phillips, AFSB, President, Phillips Insurance, Chicopee, MA

Chris-Michael Carangelo has always been a consummate professional. A go-getter who has a clear understanding of the sales lifecycle. I enjoyed working with him on projects where we had clients in common.

Susan Harper, Owner, Sharper Creative, LLC, Holtwood, PA

LIFE
OF A
SALESPERSON

Understanding the Dynamics of Selling,
Navigating Effectively Through the Process,
and Developing a Practical Mindset

CHRIS-MICHAEL CARANGELO

ISBN 979-8-9890493-0-1 (Paperback)
ISBN 979-8-9890493-1-8 (e-Book)
ISBN 979-8-9890493-2-5 (audio Book)

First Printing

Editor: **Catherine Leek of Green Onion Publishing**
Cover and Interior Design and Layout: **Kim Monteforte of Kim Monteforte Book Design & Self-Publishing Services**

Printed in USA.

This book is dedicated to all those people who get out there in the field, make the effort, have the courage to ask and make it through to success.

CONTENTS

PEOPLE NEED TO BE ASKED

Let me start by explaining how I learned that I enjoyed selling and had the ability to sell. Perhaps you too can identify an "awakening" moment in your life that gave you the motivation to pursue your future direction.

My father was a photographer by trade. He worked for Polaroid for many years and when he took an early retirement, he started his own photography business. The business focused on costume photos. You may have seen these at amusement parks or in tourist areas. Basically, you dress up in costumes – gangsters, flappers, civil war soldiers, pirates, etc. – and take a photo with an appropriate backdrop.

My father mostly utilized two channels to sell these photos. One was to set up a booth at college or other public events. The photos were paid for by the organizers. Guests at these affairs would get a free photo as a gift and thank-you for attending. The second way he sold these photos was to set up retail stores, primarily at beaches. These were open storefronts along the "strip" where he had different settings, such as an old-time saloon or a rock star stage.

When we first started out, my father and I would simply sit at the store and wait. We did not actively sell. Sales were generated when someone walked over to our store and asked. Our thought process was, "This is such a good idea, people will be excited to take an old-time photo." We figured they would absolutely "flock" into our store.

Unfortunately, sales were mediocre at best. It started to get depressing because it seemed no one was interested. People would simply walk by and look at us like we were mannequins. Some people would stop, but then immediately move on to the next store or arcade game.

One day I noticed this young guy operating one of the arcade games near our store. You know, the ones where you win the stuffed animal or the goofy toy? Every time someone walked by him, he would say something to them just to make conversation. But he would always follow it up by asking if they wanted to try the game. In fact, part of his sales pitch was literally, "Just a buck, what the f*&%?" I kid you not! That was his sales pitch.

It seemed that people were always playing his game and he usually made a good amount of money each day. Meanwhile, we were sitting there at our store people watching and hoping for a magical opportunity to drop into our laps.

It was then that I realized the number one principal of sales. *People need to be asked.* People are not likely to do something, especially something that costs money, unless they're asked. I learned that they needed a reason to do it, some incentive. They simply needed to be invited. I also discovered that the more people you ask, the more likely someone will eventually buy from you. I had a past manager that used the phrase, "You don't ask, you don't get." Sounds simple, right?

So, I started to put this approach into practice. I didn't always have the best opening lines, but I made sure to ask everyone walking by the store if they wanted to get a picture taken. Then, I would say things like, their girlfriend would love them more, they would be famous or something silly – you know, the incentive thing. It started to work well. More and more people came into the store, dressed up in the costumes and bought photos. As I became more skilled, I started offering two-for-one deals. Sure enough, sales increased considerably.

The moral of this story? In sales, a simple task repeated over and over again will produce better results. It showed me that if you ask enough people, a percentage of them will buy from you. It was easy math, a simple science, *not* a big secret. At that time, I wasn't experienced or sophisticated enough to come up with ratios or a strategy or conduct extensive research on opportunities. I learned, however, that it was merely a matter of effort and that there was no "magic" trick to selling as I had once thought.

Now, if I could impart one major takeaway for you after reading *Life of a Salesperson*, it is this. If you prepare yourself mentally, are willing to work hard, make the right decisions, be humble and patient, learn from both success and failure and stay determined, you will succeed.

Notice, I didn't ask you to attend my make-over-a-million-in-a-month seminar and pay $200.

GREAT MENTORS MATTER

Of notable importance to me is how I first learned how to sell, as you read in my opening story (page xi).

I must tell you up front that there is no get rich quick scheme and no script that tells you what to say and be guaranteed success in two weeks. *Life of a Salesperson* was written to prepare you mentally and mechanically for your journey. You will be able to walk through the sales process and make sure you are working as efficiently and effectively as possible while creating realistic expectations along the way.

I've had a great career in sales and marketing and have closed some very lucrative deals. I have also had my share of losses and disappointments.

As far as my own experience goes, I've been a salesperson in two industries: insurance and advertising. As you read through this book, you will see that my examples come mainly from those two areas of expertise. My working experience comes from actual selling, sales management and marketing. I did sell spreadsheet software for a week, but suddenly realized back then I had no idea what a spreadsheet was. Hey, I was young.

As my sales career developed and evolved, I picked up little things here and there and came to understand that the best teachers to learn from are those who have done well in the skill you are attempting to master. So, I tried to align myself with mentors I felt would help me become the best salesperson I could.

During the beginning of my sales career, I can't tell you how many times I sat with salespeople in presentations and watched how they sold, what they said and how they handled winning and losing situations.

After a few years, I finally got the chance to fly solo, or at least lead the sales process with a team. Now, I'm at a point where I can pull three decades of experience together and be the mentor to others.

What I have laid out in the pages of *Life of a Salesperson* are proven strategies and methods I learned and used to secure most of my sales. I'm not going to give you a bunch of bull about how I've won this award and was recognized in that journal, etc. To me, that won't matter to you if you are struggling. If anything, I hope that if you are in a slump, you will realize you are not alone. We've all been there. Some may not be as open as others about that.

The ultimate aim of *Life of a Salesperson* is to identify, analyze and develop the steps in *your* sales process. This is the primary key to increasing your likelihood of success. Where you are most likely to succeed lies in learning and successfully navigating through the sales process. This is the primary focus of this book.

Sales is a science that entails a coordinated, quantifiable strategy that continually tests hypotheses to gauge your success. The science of sales also works to match the opportunity to the seller in the most effective and efficient way possible. In other words, the opportunities are there, but you have to know how to reach them and that is what makes it a science.

Sales is also an art and I won't deny that. It does take a trustworthy, empathic and generally likeable personality to engage with your prospects. It also takes a person who can be flexible dealing with different personality types. Personality and approach is a definite added bonus. But you won't be able to perform your art if you haven't scientifically found the right opportunity.

So, let's begin with a general outline that will help you create the most effective strategy.

Mental Preparation

- Put on your game face.
- Prepare for a long-term journey.

Objective – Be in the Right Place at the Right Time

- Create a strategy that directs you to the right people, in the right places, when they are in need of your product or service.

Research and Determine Your Best Audience

- Accept the actual audience versus the desired audience.
- Do the prep work.
- Analyze your existing customer base.
- Generate a qualified lead list.
- Objective: Find the most likely, highest valued opportunities in the shortest amount of time.
- Analyze your competition.
- Map out a plan of attack.

Don't Take It Personally; It's All in the Ratios

- Identifying the Sales Ratios determines the amount of work it takes to get a sale.
- Know the factors affecting your ratios.
- Learn to improve these ratios.
- Rejection has to do more with situation than you.

Prospecting Objective

- Sell to get an appointment, not to blither out information.
- Follow up, follow up, follow up.
- Never call to confirm an appointment.
- Have a prepared strategy to handle objections.

The Discovery Meeting

- Reach the decision-maker. Don't settle for less.
- Analyze the technical aspects of your prospect as well as their level of commitment.
- Don't be afraid to walk away if there's no opportunity.
- Learn the signs of opportunity as well as dead-end initiatives.

Your Presentation and Closing

- Turn the needs and pain points learned in your Discovery Meeting into the primary items you address in your solution.
- Identify those specific needs/pain points and how you will address them.
- Identify and explain any areas you have discovered that the prospect may not have known about.

At the end of your presentation, ensure you will be able to show that you have listened, that you have weighed your alternatives and that you have come up with the most effective strategy or products to meet the needs and concerns they stated.

Constantly Monitor Your Progress

- Review your ratios.
- Consider your "pitch."
- Review your Discovery Meeting questions and answers.
- Analyze how and why you won and lost sales.
- Consider changing your target audiences or putting more effort into the successful efforts.

In a nutshell, the key to better success is to have a plan, a strategy, an objective and effective execution and a way to monitor progress. Your overall strategy should be thought of like a military plan. All aspects are considered. Intelligence is gathered and research analyzed. Your execution has a focus and an objective. You are prepared for obstacles. And you will deliver with great precision and, most of all, confidence.

Let's start building that plan!

1

CREATING THE RIGHT MINDSET

"Let me tell you something you already know. The world ain't all sunshine and rainbows. It's a very mean and nasty place and I don't care how tough you are it will beat you to your knees if you let it. You, me or nobody is gonna hit as hard as life. But it ain't about how hard you hit. It's about how hard you can get hit and keep moving forward. How much you can take and keep moving forward. That's how winning is done!"

—SYLVESTER STALLONE, *ROCKY BALBOA* (2006)

So, you decided to take a shot at sales? You think you have what it takes and wish to pursue a new career. Perhaps you have been selling for some time and need to fine tune some skills. Maybe you have been trying to sell but you're hitting some roadblocks and looking for some help. Maybe, perhaps, you have been successful in your sales journey but want to continue learning more and sharpening your skills as many experienced, diligent salespeople do.

Here's the good news. If you have had any sales experience at all, you've probably been in at least one of the scenarios described above.

That is why it is so important to step back every now and then, understand what you are involved in and accept and embrace the magnitude of your endeavor.

Mental Preparation

Sales is a rewarding occupation. You can make a ton of money and live a decent life selling products and services. The great thing about sales is you are in control of your own income. You won't have to plod through a year, waiting to see if your boss likes you enough to give you a minimal raise. You also won't have to hope that the company as a whole did well enough that you might get a .000001% bonus. In sales, if you make a sale, you get paid. Period. The more sales you make, the more money you make. Period.

IN SALES, IF YOU MAKE A SALE, YOU GET PAID. PERIOD.

On the flip side, sales can also be stressful. It takes a lot of hard work along with crucial decision-making and time management skills. You need to develop a thick skin and learn not to take things personally. Worry not, however, because we are going to walk through the areas of sales that cause such stress and help you learn to make wise, crucial decisions and develop that so-called "thick skin" you need.

Regardless of whether or not sales is rewarding or stressful, the one thing sales is not is easy. Sales is not a get-rich quick process, a thirty-minute infomercial or pyramid scheme. Let's get that out of your mind right now. If the people touting these concepts are successful, then why are they trying to sell their idea and getting you to join their network? If they were that successful, they would be selling their product or service and not trying to recruit people to sell for them.

In fact, if there's one thing I can't stand it's when "that guy" calls me up, approaches me in church or at a party and tells me he has a tremendous "business opportunity." Yes! When I was naïve and hungry with very little sales experience, I'd inquire about such a fantastic idea! Then, I learned the hard truth.

It was never about selling a product or service. It was about getting me to join their little network and then convincing others to do the same. I would then have to offer this same "business opportunity" to other people and, believe me, this is a great way to repel friends and family. It was also a ridiculous proposal. It was like, "Hey, Uncle John! Why don't you leave your lucrative profession as a surgeon and join my network to sell dishes and razors." You get what I'm saying here?

All good things in life, if they are worthy, take time and effort to pursue. Unfortunately, we now live in an instant gratification society and we've lost the concept of long-term achievements and the persever-ance that goes with it. As a salesperson, therein lies your challenge. If you are willing to embrace the concept of long-term goals, strengthen your mental stamina, have patience and do the hard work, you will be able to move forward in your sales career.

When I played hockey as a kid, I remember my father telling me over and over again, "Sports is 85% attitude, 15% aptitude." You can argue the percentages of this, but you can't argue the need to have the right attitude regardless of talent. There will be times when your attitude, if negative, will cost you a sale simply because you won't believe in your success. It's important to stay positive and realize that someone else succeeded in this profession, so you can too.

Having said all of this, let's start developing a realistic, but confident attitude right now. Before you even begin your sales career or move any further into it, you will need to mentally prepare by creating some realistic expectations.

Settle This in Your Mind

Settling the following things in your mind ahead of time will equip you far more potently for the future. If you commit to understanding and accepting the reality of your sales endeavor now, when those times of struggle come you will not be as discouraged. In fact, you will be more ready to take on the challenges. You will also be able to handle your success. Yes, it's true. Some people do not handle success well. So, let's go through some of these expectations and establish a healthy mindset.

Selling Is Not Easy

I expect most professionals would also agree that their occupations require effort, but to be successful in sales requires patience, diligence and courage.

- It will take time for you to build a client base and/or a book of business.
- You will have both successes and setbacks. Notice, I didn't say failure. You will learn from your setbacks.
- You need to think long term. This is a marathon, not a sprint.
- You will need to ask, ask, ask and understand that most likely people will say no more than yes.
- You will need to pick up the phone and/or walk into businesses. You have to deal directly with people, and you can't hide behind social media or email.
- It will take longer for you to get a sale up front, simply because it takes experience to become more efficient.
- You may have to work extra hours, nights and weekends. Again, this will happen more at the beginning simply because you will be hungry.
- Some prospects will lie to you, lead you on or, worse, shut you down during the process.

The Stresses

It may sound negative, but realistically, every occupation has its stresses. Just be thankful you're not a politician, surgeon or a judge. At least you're not making laws that put people in jail or could take their lives.

- There is a stigma attached to salespeople. It's an unfair assumption, but some people will look at you as slimy, think you are using them or you want something from them. In fact, I learned a funny word over the years describing salespeople. The word is "smarmy." Look that one up.

- People may not want to be around you if they know you are a salesperson. This, however, assumes what you sell involves them.

- They believe that you need to be more aggressive than your competitors to win.

When you finally land a sale, everything listed above will be offset and overcome by the joy and excitement of closing the deal. In other words, the sale overcomes all of the pain and frustration derived from the obstacles it took to get you there.

The Upside

Nevertheless, sales has huge benefits. You can certainly succeed. As I said before, landing a sale can be exhilarating. Successes will grow over time and you will get better at it as you gain experience. Try to think of these examples to get into the right mindset.

- When you work out in a gym consistently, over time you will become more muscular and be in better shape.

- If you constantly practice hitting a baseball, over time your batting average will improve.

- If you study hard, you will pass your test, get your degree and most likely land a lucrative career.

- If you do your research and have patience, when you invest in the stock market, your money will grow over time.

These things don't happen overnight. Yet, they do happen. Your sales success will be similar. The more effort you put into it, the better you will become.

So, now that we've covered the pros and cons of selling, let's assume you have made your decision to move forward (or continue). If this is you, then it's time to get ready and put on your game face.

Putting on Your Game Face

Have you ever played in a competitive sport? Or participated in a music competition, spelling bee or some kind of trivia game? If you have ever been in any type of contest, you may have felt the adrenaline rush that comes with playing to win. It's an exhilarating feeling that consumes your mind and body, motivating you to give nothing short of your best in a given situation. Conducting military operations as well will do this.

Let's go a step further. Suppose that the game you were playing in was some kind of playoff or championship. It might be the end of a tournament, or the end of the season, the finals.

Let's go even further. Suppose there was even more on the line for you and your team. What if you were representing your school in a State Championship? What if you were representing your country in the Olympics? The victory would not just mean a lot to you. It would also mean a great deal to those people who supported you and believed in you. It could mean simply pride, legacy or perhaps great posterity. These are the times you put on your game face.

YOUR "GAME FACE" IS THAT POINT WHEN YOU HAVE DETERMINED BOTH MENTALLY AND PHYSICALLY THAT YOU WILL NOT FAIL.

Your "game face" is that point when you have determined both mentally and physically that you will not fail. Period. You decide you will put your heart and soul into whatever you are doing, and that failure is not an option. You will concentrate, pray, meditate, be as disciplined and determined as you need to be to carry out your best possible outcome. In essence, you have made a decision for yourself to win and you will do whatever it takes to stay committed to that decision. It is giving nothing short of your absolute best. You're all in. Peak performance.

Does this sound hokey to you? Well, perhaps you could ask the 1980 USA Hockey Team (Miracle on Ice). They were a college-level hockey team taking on the best professional players in the Soviet Union (Russia). They were huge underdogs and never expected to win. Yet, they did. It was the biggest upset in sports history.

How about asking the 2004 Boston Red Sox? The Boston Red Sox had multiple opportunities to win a World Series but went eighty-six years without taking home the pennant. It was called "The Curse of the Bambino." In order to win the World Series, the 2004 Red Sox needed to win the league championship. They had to come back from a series deficit of 3-0 against their super arch-rival, the New York Yankees. The Yankees crushed the Red Sox for many years prior. Yet this Red Sox team believed they could both win everything and overcome that dreaded mental obstacle known as the curse. They came back to win this series and went on to sweep the Saint Louis Cardinals in the finals and became the 2004 World Series Champions.

How about one last example? Let's ask the 20th Maine Regiment of Union Soldiers how they overcame insurmountable odds on Little Round Top in Gettysburg during the Civil War. These guys are true heroes because they were given an order to fight "at all hazards." This means they were ordered to either fight against the Confederates, right there, or die. If they lost that battle, the Confederates would have swept the entire Union line and we might just be living in two countries right now. Yet, those men gave it all. They put on their game face and won.

There are instances in your life when you have no choice but to win. Your sales career has to be thought of like that. You are going to put considerable time and effort into your sales career and you are sacrificing other opportunities to do this. To fail means you will have to quit and start another career all over again. You will have lost money and time and your self-esteem will take a significant blow.

I'll add a small disclaimer to this, however. There are times when your product, service or company are just not needed and no matter what you or they do, success will be unattainable. These are setbacks for you, not utter failures. You give up when you quit for good. Otherwise, learn and grow. But always be ready. Be ready to win.

2

ESTABLISHING THE RIGHT STRATEGY

"I have observed something else under the sun. The fastest runner doesn't always win the race, and the strongest warrior doesn't always win the battle. The wise sometimes go hungry, and the skillful are not necessarily wealthy. And those who are educated don't always lead successful lives. It is all decided by chance, by being in the right place at the right time."

—ECCLESIASTES 9:11

The Right Place at the Right Time

This quote from Solomon, the wisest man in the world according to the Old Testament, lays out a very profound notion that applies to many areas of life. Success comes from being in the right place at the right time. This should be the core belief for your sales career. Grasping this observation provides you with a realistic focus when creating and developing your overall sales strategy.

SALES IS MORE ABOUT THE SITUATION THAN ANYTHING ELSE.

Let's put Solomon's quote in simpler and more specific terms. *Sales is more about the situation than anything else.* This is why your overall, general objective in selling will be to skillfully find ways to land you in the right place at the right time.

It's Not Always About You

As a salesperson you need to understand and practice this discipline. Yes, your charisma and charm can have an impact on landing an opportunity. You can persuade that CEO or COO to make a decision and go with your product. However, the problem is that many times, no matter how much a prospect likes you, no matter how funny you are or even how boring you are, the time and circumstance has to be right for a prospect to move forward. You must train yourself to work within such given circumstances and, most often, override your emotions.

Let me give you a typical insurance-related example. Most businesses buy insurance for a full year term because most policies last one year at a time. When insurance policies come up for renewal, the insured will either decide to renew their policies with their current agent and/or company or shop around for better coverage and pricing.

If they decide to shop around, the remarketing process can take between thirty and one-hundred-and-twenty days to find suitable alternatives. The remarketing process consists of gathering information, possibly conducting inspections for loss control, generating applications, finding a competitive, willing insurance company to write the business, etc. For the insurance salesperson, the key objective is to find out when a business or organization's insurance policies renew and contact them early enough so they will be willing to let you remarket their insurance.

Nowadays, limited policy renewal information is available in some form through state bureaus or other lead generating sources. However, if that information is not available to you, you must start generating a renewal date database. As there are twelve months in a year, and numerous businesses to contact, building such a list increases the chances of catching this business at the right time.

That's why it may take an insurance salesperson one to two years to amass a qualified base of prospects and it takes far more calls in the beginning to build up your renewal list.

Not that it's impossible, but it is rare that an insurance salesperson is going to contact a business outside of their renewal term and convince the company to buy from them. It happens, but you can't live on it.

The point is, a prospect may think you're funny, good-looking, smart, etc., but they may not be in a position to buy from you at a particular time.

Another typical problem occurs for many sales professionals who sell to businesses – trying to "pitch" a neighborhood business that is a franchise or part of a chain. The local owner might be your friend, neighbor, etc., but the corporate office in East Nowhere, Idaho, handles the contracts or buying decisions for the product/service you are selling. Thus, you would have to either make a phone call or take a trip to Idaho to try to get this business. The further away, generally speaking, the less likely are your chances of success.

Many times, businesses deal with friends and relatives. You may have heard that dopey "Cousin Bob handles all of our IT issues," or "Earl, a guy I know at my church that I want to support even though he's horrible at fixing my office equipment." Again, to buy from you, M. Charismatic Salesperson, would cause a rift in a friendship or someone could be ostracized from their family.

You get the point, I'm sure. It's a situation that you might not be able to change, but it's not something your personality can do anything about.

There are numerous other times where the situation or circumstance first and foremost simply prohibits the prospect from even considering what you have to offer. This is why it's important to identify the right opportunities as opposed to finding just people who like you. This way you will end up in the right place at the right time.

What's a good, efficient salesperson to do? To start, you must learn the intricacies of the process your product or service is involved in.

- How and when do people purchase?
- Is it a lengthy process?
- Is it a bidding process as many government entities coordinate?
- Is there a trend in a particular industry that buyers, for example, go to their trade organization for help?

Let's delve deeper. Being in the right place at the right time also means you need to get to the decision-maker. This is paramount because far more often than not, if you don't reach the decision-maker, you will not get a decision and that, ultimately, is a big, fat disappointing no.

BEING IN THE RIGHT PLACE AT THE RIGHT TIME ALSO MEANS YOU NEED TO GET TO THE DECISION-MAKER.

Where is this decision-maker? Experienced people know exactly where they are. They're in a meeting. They're golfing. They're taking the kids to the doctor today. They're on the phone at the moment and will call you back. They're away on a business trip and will return in two weeks. Experienced salespeople are actually surprised when that one in one hundred decision-maker is actually right there, ready to speak with them.

The key strategy here is activity. Yes, this is why your sales manager is all over you asking what you did this week? An increase in your activities, such as calls, door-to-door visits, trade association meetings, correspondingly increases the chances you will get in touch with the person you need to speak with.

Your activities also need to be relevant, however. Talking to the wait staff at a chamber of commerce meeting is not a real activity. And, no, neither is chatting with the bartender (we've all been there).

Eighth Time Is the Charm

Let me give you a real scenario of what I'm talking about. I once had an experience where it took eight attempts to reach the person I knew I needed to reach. I was trying to sell some digital advertising to a local motorcycle dealership. I needed to reach their internal Marketing Manager. Here's how the play went.

First call, he was unavailable. Second call, he was out of the office. Third contact, which was a walk-in, he was in a meeting. Fourth contact, another walk-in visit, he simply was not there. When I got to the eighth try, I happened to be sitting in a Dairy Queen eating an ice cream across the street from this business. I was heading back to the office and I thought, "What the heck, I'll try one more time."

I crossed the street, walked into the dealership and low and behold, to my amazement the Marketing Manager was actually on the sales floor talking to one of his salespeople. I literally yelled out, "JD! How are you doing? I've been trying to contact you! Do you have a minute?" Note that I didn't really care what his answer was, I would have tackled him if he walked away. I worked hard to get to the point to at least give my pitch and I was going to give it.

To make a long story short, I got my chance to pitch my offerings and set up an appointment. Subsequently, we had our appointment, went through the entire sales cycle and this turned out to be one of my largest sales in my advertising career. The lesson I learned here was to conduct activities that successfully put me in the right place at the right time.

Let's dive even further. This time, we'll throw in a caveat. Perhaps you got to the right person at the right time, but the value of this prospect is minimal. Suppose you are targeting machine shops and you called and called and called and finally reached the owner. You now meet with the owner and discover that it's a small shop with three employees. You went through all of that effort for little potential reward.

Step one is to get yourself in the right place at the right time.

Step two – and this is an important caveat – you must look for the *most likely, highest valued opportunities in the shortest amount of time.*

These objectives will be covered in more depth in the next chapter, and throughout this book, but it's crucial to drill down into this concept as well. Remember this! It serves as an important guide when making decisions, especially strategic or quick decisions that require wisdom. You want to be in the right place at the right time *for the best opportunities.*

3

UNDERSTANDING YOUR OBJECTIVE

"Balance is not something you find, it's something you create."

—JANA KINGSFORD

You have your sales mindset established – you are mentally prepared for the journey. The concept of being in the right place at the right time will form the basis of your overall strategy toward selling. But what is your objective? What is your goal?

To make a sale, to earn the dollars – obviously. But how do you reach your target? How can we put that objective into practice?

You want to find the *most likely, highest valued prospects in the shortest amount of time.* You need to discover the features of the clients most likely to purchase from you – are they local, are they the experts targeted to use your product/service, do you share some sort of connection, etc.?

From this list of most likely buyers, you need to next determine who are the highest valued prospects. This could be the one that will bring in the most revenue. But it might also be the one you have the closest connection with and can make the sale quickly and with less effort. Making this decision will require some calculating.

And finally, you want to complete the transaction in the shortest amount of time possible. This objective might seem obvious, but there can be a number of scheduling factors that come into play.

Through experience, you will also learn when and how you will need to balance these three objectives. Let's start with exploring the qualities and attributes of your most likely candidates.

Most Likely Prospects

Your most likely prospects are the ones you will have the most advantage with or the best chance of securing. This comes from your realistic position of strength. For example, if your organization sells mostly to companies who favor doing business locally, then you may want to start by focusing on prospects within a local radius, say twenty-five miles from your location.

Or, let's say your company has an expertise serving auto-related businesses such as repair shops. You have a solid base of these businesses and they view you as a premier vendor. Your good reputation in this arena gives you an advantage. In this case, targeting such a niche would make sense.

Many times, however, the most likely prospects come from a combination of variables. So, let's examine a list of characteristics that could put them in your "most likely" category.

Local Presence

As much as the world is becoming more technical and social-media oriented, there is still a gravitational pull for many business owners to center their custom around being local. This applies more, perhaps, the further you are located from a big city. Why?

Many people who live in suburbs and rural areas have lived there for a long time. Or, they moved away from a big city because they prefer the suburban/rural lifestyle. Consequently, they want to preserve their suburban or rural culture by supporting local people. Many times, as well, since communities are smaller, friendships tend to be more frequent and long term. So not only are they supporting their community, but they may also feel like they are supporting their friends.

As I mentioned before, I've gotten my foot in the door and have landed many sales based on my "local" pitch more than my actual "products and services highlights" pitch. Being local creates a bond and definitely gives you an advantage – and advantage is what gives you a higher likelihood of securing their business.

ADVANTAGE IS WHAT GIVES YOU A HIGHER LIKELIHOOD OF SECURING THEIR BUSINESS.

Specialty or Expertise

References matter. Experience matters. Seriously, if you were putting an addition on your house, would you want someone who had two months of construction experience with no completed jobs to show for it, or would you hire an experienced contractor with a strong portfolio of completed projects and a good number of references?

Well, if you want to take the cheap way out, you'd go with the former, but you'll probably be nervous about it and calling the person back for do-overs or to make corrections. On the other hand, you might pay more for the experience, but you also gain peace of mind knowing and trusting that the job was done right. Therein lies your advantage.

If your company or you personally have experience in a given industry or area of expertise, you will be able to tout that knowledge to a prospect and provide references that will back up your case. What distinguishes specialty and expertise from a local presence is specialty can exceed the boundaries of being local. Local is confined to a given area, but you can expand as far as you'd like using the expertise advantage.

Connection and Relationship

The Bible talks about different kinds of love: *Eros, Thanatos* and *Philos*. For this purpose, we will look at *Philos*, which is commonly referred to as "brotherly love" or having a "common bond." What we are looking at here is commonality.

I'm going to get a little politically incorrect here and say something that is perhaps controversial, but nevertheless true. It's something you may or may not care about. Regardless, you will not be able to change this dynamic in a sales capacity without losing money.

Like kind buys from like kind. This could mean a number of things, but in general, it is the thing that bonds people together. It is these types of personal connections that give you advantage. Here are some examples.

- Belonging to a local group such as a Chamber of Commerce, Rotary or other type of industrial group.
- Family relationship – brother, sister, second-cousin, tenth cousin-once removed, whatever. It's the "blood is thicker than water" thing. Turning down a relative for business doesn't always sit well at Thanksgiving meals.
- Same political beliefs. Who wants to meet up with a salesperson and argue over politics? Unless you are selling to a given political organization, *never* mention politics and dissuade people from getting into such discussions.

  I can never understand why Hollywood people spout their political ideologies when their audiences come from such different beliefs. They shoot themselves in the foot by alienating parts of their audience when they get into politics. And they have no expertise in that area. Just do your job! The same goes for professional athletes. Stick to your core business and stay away from political discussions.

  Nevertheless, if you are known for your beliefs, you will more likely find advantage with a like-minded prospect, than you will selling to someone with opposing views.

Religious Beliefs

Believe it or not, some people have strong convictions about doing business only with the people from their religion. I have no exact numbers to prove this. Although having tried to sell to the Amish and Mennonite communities in Pennsylvania, I can tell you that it was extremely hard to make that first step simply because they tended to stay within their own people.

Again, however, if you have similar beliefs, it gives you an advantage. There are Christians who buy from Christians, Jews who buy from Jews, Muslims who buy from Muslims, etc.

Race or Nationality

You can hide this fact in society, but you'd be a fool to deny it in sales. You will lose money if you do. Remember, like kind buys from like kind. Not always, of course, as we don't want to stereotype, but the tendency is there. Italians buy from Italians, Irish buy from Irish, Jewish buy from Jewish, Indian people buy from Indian people, etc.

I believe, though, the reasons are more positive than negative. People have tendencies to trust people who are more like them. They also want to support people like them. Like it or not, it happens. I don't think it's a terrible thing, but it does sometimes get in the way of a prospect finding the best alternatives for their business.

We are not selling social activism so let other people change these things if they don't like them. You just need to navigate your sales strategy within this dynamic (if it exists) so that you can create advantage.

Other

There could be a whole host of other advantages, such as the fact that you went to high school or college together. Or you grew up in the same town. Or you both prefer iPhones over Androids.

In essence, the connection is that personal belief or ideal that you find is important to a prospect. Once you have identified it, you can then use your similar belief or idea as a way to persuade your prospect that you can be trusted because of your common bond.

I mentioned this wasn't going to be politically correct, which is why I say keep the politics out of it. The goal is to identify the dynamic and learn to maneuver wisely through it.

Need

Need is the most important connection you could make. Need is also the toughest connection you can make up front when trying to get your foot in the door. However, once you are able to gain access and diagnose the needs of your prospect, the need connection becomes more evident.

Initially, the problem is identifying the specific need of your prospect. Sometimes, you might be able to find a void in a given industry that your product fulfills. Take a specific product, like insurance coverage for plumbers, as an example. If your insurance policy covers faulty plumbing work specifically, and your competition does not, and you find that is a real need for plumbing contractors, your need lead-in can create a connection.

Need is also the most realistic. Regardless of whether or not you belong to the same church or went to the same college, if you can't meet the prospects' needs, then they can't – or won't – do business with you.

Suppose you are suffering from depression and anxiety and you are searching out a psychologist for help. You might meet with two or three to see which one will work best for you. Of the three you meet, you might like the first one best from a personality standpoint and you seem to click with that person more than the others. However, that doctor does not specialize or have much experience with depression and anxiety whereas the other two are actually specialists in your area of need.

As much as you like the first doctor, they will not be able to best meet your need. So, you will have to choose one of the other two.

In a nutshell, your aim is to always strive to identify the need either before or after you've gotten your foot in the door. Without knowledge of that specific need, however, you can at least make some kind of connection with your prospect with the goal of securing an appointment. Nevertheless, identifying a prospect's real need is paramount.

Highest Valued Prospects

You would think this is a no-brainer, and from a numbers standpoint it is. If Prospect A will bring in $10,000 in revenue and Prospects B and C will bring in $5,000, you target Prospect A first. Right?

But what happens when you add Most Likely, Highest Valued to the equation? Suppose Prospect A is a partner member in a Chamber of Commerce that you just met and Prospect B is a friend you grew up with and Prospect C goes to your church? Now you have to balance this equation further.

Adding to your challenge is the sales goal you need to reach. If your goal is $10,000, do you strive for Prospect A, who will get you to that target in one sale, or try for B and C?

Granted, anything is possible, but the meaning of highest valued is that you strive to get the most you can in your situation.

Through experience, however, and constant activity, you will be able to better identify where your higher valued prospects are. Once identified, you can weigh your chances of success in securing these sales and it will eventually help you balance your most likely/highest valued equation.

The best way to avoid the dilemma of having to make this determination on the spot is to do your research beforehand. If you are good at selling computer networks to wholesalers, and this is a specialty for your company, they may have already targeted the firms in a given area and secured some of the larger wholesalers. You would then either have to expand the territory to reach other large clients or settle for the smaller ones within your territory that were not pursued initially.

THE IMPORTANCE OF QUANTIFYING THE VALUE OF YOUR PROSPECTS IS CRUCIAL TO REACH YOUR GOAL.

Without a doubt, the importance of quantifying the value of your prospects is crucial to reach your goal.

In the Shortest Amount of Time

Usually, the larger the client, the longer it will take to actually go through the process and close a sale. Many times, larger companies have multiple decision-makers or decision-makers that need influencers present, such as department managers or people with specific skill sets. You may have to gather more information through multiple channels and, ultimately, in order to make a final decision there may be a chain of command or vote needed. Conversely, a "Mom and Pop" shop might be run by one person who can meet and reach a decision right away.

That's one part of timing. The other part of timing has to do with the type of product or service you are selling. In insurance, as I mentioned before, the renewal or effective date of the policies creates the sales cycle and initiates the process. Thus, you might have a viable prospect, but will have to wait until their policies renew to begin the sales process. Other businesses might have contracts, such as advertising, accounting services, etc., that also have an expiration date.

This does bring up another point, which is part of your sales pitch. Many times, when a cold call is made, a prospect might say no because of the timing. If that is the issue, a great follow up is to ask when their contract or service expires and do they, or will they, look for alternatives when that happens? Then, you can nail down a date and conduct a more qualified follow-up. You can even remind the prospect during that follow-up call that they asked you to call them again, breaking that unfamiliarity they had with you at first. "Remember when we spoke back in September? You told me to give you a call now and you'd be willing to discuss" – that kind of approach.

Nevertheless, timing is everything. You may have multiple, likely prospects with varying values, but if one is coming up soon and they will help you meet or exceed your goal, then timing becomes primary.

The question becomes which one do you target first? For this answer, I will provide two schools of thought to consider as your approach.

The first one uses a financial concept known as the "Time Value of Money." This idea states that cash in hand now is better than cash to be received in the future, because cash in hand can also earn interest. Putting this in sales terms? Your goal would be to always get the sale that you can close sooner. This approach is great when you have a strong pipeline, and you are confident you are going to reach your goals. In this case, your "Cash" is the actual sale you land. The "Interest" is the time you can now spend on other prospects since you were able to land this sale more quickly. Basically, it's an efficient use of your time.

The second school of thought is to target the sales that meet a specific objective. Having a sales goal is usually the reason to implement this approach. I'll give you a scenario.

Let's say you are $5,000 below goal and you have two weeks left in the month. You have Prospect A, a moderately likely candidate valued at $10,000. Prospect B is highly likely and valued at $5,000. Prospect C is also highly likely and valued at $5,000. Let's add to this equation now.

Prospect A is not in a hurry and you secured this contender in the middle of a contract term, so there is time. Prospect B is at the renewal stage of a contract and Prospect C has no contract and no timeline.

This is where your experience comes in. Which sale would you try to close first? Then second?

My choice would be Prospect B first since there is a deadline, they are highly likely to buy and the $5,000 value will achieve my goal. I'd probably shoot for Prospect C next to exceed the goal, but if I can't get the sale in this month from C, it will at least help next month. Then, if I have time, I'll go after A.

You might differ. You might just go for Prospect A thinking you can meet and exceed your goal in one shot. You might go for C first because there is no timeline, and you could secure it tomorrow. What I want to get across is that time is an important consideration in the equation, and you need to weigh it properly. You, however, will learn and gain knowledge of your own situations.

Another aspect of timing has to do with the time of year. In advertising, for example, the heavier months are during holiday seasons. So, September, October, November and December are great months for Thanksgiving, Christmas, Hannukah, New Years, etc. Businesses love to advertise during the holiday season so your likelihood of securing qualified prospects increases. On the other hand, a slower month might be after June or in August, as there are not as many holidays and people take vacations during the summer months. Securing qualified leads either takes more effort or you may have to settle for less during this time.

We will talk about how to manage such "seasonal" changes later (in Chapter 5), but this needs to be considered because you may have to exceed a goal during a peak to make up for the slower months.

4

DEFINING AND REACHING YOUR BEST AUDIENCE

"Success is where preparation and opportunity meet."

—BOBBY UNSER, NASCAR DRIVER

Ever hear of the expression, "He's running around like a chicken with its head cut off?" I've never seen a chicken running around with its head cut off in real life, but I do know what kills so many sales careers. It's a lack of direction and no plan of attack.

Prep Work Is Vital to Success

Prior to getting into my insurance career, I worked in various areas of construction, including steel work, masonry and general contracting. For the most part, being younger and starting out I was mostly labor, helping the contractors and completing small jobs. What I learned from working in construction was a great lesson that I eventually carried into sales.

At one specific time, I worked for a residential mason who did mostly ornamental jobs such as stairs, chimneys and walls. Our jobs were smaller and lasted usually a week or two at the most.

If you were to take a snapshot of a mason working, it might look like they just showed up and started laying bricks – kind of like playing with Lego®, only heavier. It might even look easy and fast because they do get the job done swiftly. However, they are able to complete their job quickly and with high quality because of the preparations made beforehand.

One of the hardest days I ever worked in my life was when I was working for that masonry company and we built a large stone wall for a local homeowner. The first day of this particular job started at 5:00 a.m. and lasted fifteen hours.

The initial task was to go to the local quarry and purchase the stone. The two masons, my co-worker who was also a laborer and I made five trips to the quarry. At each visit, the masons inspected each rock that they wanted us to use and instructed us to load these chosen stones onto the truck. Mind you, these were not small rocks. Each one weighed between ten to one hundred pounds. Once these rocks were gathered and delivered to the job site, we had to buy the cement and sand. This was not easy either as each bag weighed at least fifty pounds. At least the sand needed was dumped into and out of the mason's truck. We also brought a mixer from the owner's garage.

Once all of the materials were gathered and delivered, we began to prepare the area where the wall was going to be built. We started by digging out the footing. Next, the masons measured what they needed to and we put up the measuring strings. We also built the foundations with wood so we could pour cement in the footing. That was day one.

On day two, everything was in place and ready to go. So, we began to mix the cement and the masons were able to build the wall in about ten hours. Our job as laborers was to mix the cement and bring the rocks to the wall. If you were to show up the second day, you would think the work was actually fun because it looked so easy and was moving along rather steadily.

The point of telling this story is to point out that, much like the preparation in construction, your preparation and research beforehand are vital to your sales success. Failure to prepare becomes a trial-and-error endeavor that you might as well refer to as an error-by-error endeavor.

One perfect example deals with cold calling. If you need to make one hundred phone calls a week, you can't just pick up the phone and start dialing businesses without knowing anything about them. That would be like building the wall and having to continuously find your materials during the process, not being sure if they are even the right materials.

You might spend hours trying just to get in touch with people who are either not a good prospect for you or simply the wrong person. The opportunity lost from doing this is devastating. At the very least, if you're going to make one hundred calls, call the people you have the best chance with. To do this, you must research who you are going to call, put your list together, import it into your database and be ready to track the progress of each call.

Therein lies your challenge. Your main sales objective at this point, as I mentioned in the prior chapter, is to find the most likely, highest valued prospect in the least amount of time.

Gathering Your Materials

Accepting Your Audience

When was the last time you went to a wedding that had a DJ? During the time you were at this wedding, did you notice whether or not the guests were dancing to the music the DJ was playing and having a good time, or were they mostly sitting around looking bored while only a handful of people danced?

I've experienced both types of weddings, among other events in which a DJ was involved. I started to observe a certain dynamic at these events. Some DJs play what *they* like to play while other DJs play what the *audience* reacts to.

So, let's say we're at a wedding and the bride and groom are relatively young, say in their 20s. Their favorite music might be rap, hip-hop or something more modern. Yet, the DJ might be a Gen-Xer, like me, and think everyone likes 80s music (granted, it was the best decade for music). However, the music is not resonating with the crowd and they are simply not participating in any dancing. But the DJ keeps playing 80s music.

Conversely, a better DJ, even though he likes 80s music realizes he was hired to please his audience. He will try different types of music from different eras and, depending on how the crowd reacts, he will adjust his playlist to reflect the music genres that get them moving.

Let's go one step further. A great DJ will inquire up front, before the gig, about the demographics of the people attending the wedding and what music will be most likely favored. Then, he will have a far better likelihood of picking the right songs and keeping the audience engaged.

Do you see how this works? The takeaway here is that there is a true discipline to accepting what your audience looks like and what they desire, versus what you like or are comfortable with. Your audience of prospects may also be similar. It may not be an audience you are comfortable with or like, but it may be the audience you are likely to get. Big difference.

IT MAY NOT BE AN AUDIENCE YOU ARE COMFORTABLE WITH OR LIKE, BUT IT MAY BE THE AUDIENCE YOU ARE LIKELY TO GET. BIG DIFFERENCE.

You might have had experience in restaurants working as a server or a cook in your prior life. You understand the operations of a restaurant and feel comfortable relating to people in that industry. However, your company does not have a product or service that meets the needs of restaurants, or the product you offer is not competitive for them. On the other hand, you do have a product that benefits contractors with an existing client base to show for it. So, your discipline will be to learn the contractor field and language, etc., so you will be able to reach that market rather than the restaurant market. It's not a comfort zone, but it is a money zone. Your sales goal is to make money, not to work for emotional comfort.

It's a hard notion to accept but as I've learned throughout life, the people who get comfortable with doing things they are not comfortable with succeed more than those who only stay in their comfort zones.

The Right Audience for Your Product

I've seen this a million times in the insurance industry. An agency hires a new producer and expects them to "just get out there and find business." Can you imagine? You work in a city with a population of 100,000 people and over 5,000 businesses and you just have to go out and find business. Granted, there may be enough business out there, but without research, preparation and a plan of attack, you will be spending vast amounts of time going down dead-end roads. You will also miss out on real opportunities.

A crucial component of being in the right place at the right time has to do with finding the right audience – that is, the right audience for what you are selling. If you want to waste time and get really frustrated, pitch your product or service to someone who really doesn't need what you have to offer. This is also a hard notion to accept. Not everyone needs what you have to offer.

I live by the principle that the less value your product or service offers, the more effort is needed to sell it. You will also find that it takes high-sales-pressure techniques to move products with little quality. For the most part, a valuable product should be able to sell itself and the salesperson simply needs to identify and recognize the value it brings to the prospect.

That's why I believe car salespeople get a bad rap. Many times, a person only wants to look at cars to get some information. The salesperson has goals, however, and needs to get you to buy something, even though you may not need a vehicle at that moment.

Or that dreaded furniture salesperson who is on you like seagulls on a French fry the minute you walk in the store! "No, I don't want to pay five thousand dollars for a sofa with plush leather imported from remote areas of Italy. I was looking for a side table. No, I don't have any questions yet, because I just got in the door! I don't even know what you sell, except that it's furniture. Leave me alone! If I need anything, I'll ask." I'm sure you have been in similar, frustrating situations.

Anyway, think about it. Learn the details and nuances of the product or service you are dealing with and the clients you will be promoting it to.

- What do you have to offer?
- Who will this benefit?
- How will it benefit them?
- Do they need what you have or do they just want it?
- And what are the features of your product or service that differentiate you from your competition?

What Do Your Existing Customers Look Like?

A great place to start to find likely prospects is to generate internal customer reports from your firm and look for patterns in the existing customer base. Do they service a lot of construction or trade businesses? Do they sell mostly to professional firms? Are they for-profit or non-profit? What size are these companies? Are they larger, smaller? How many employees? What are their annual sales? What is their SIC (Standard Industrial Classification or NAICS (North American Industry Classification System)) code?

Clues like these will help you determine your best prospects because:

1. You've already had success with these and
2. You can tout yourself, or your company, as an expert serving these types of businesses.

At the very least, you will be able to say you have familiarity with their type of business and this will give you more information to develop your plan of attack.

Dig a little deeper and find out how or why you secured these customers.

At times, it's simply price. Occasionally, it's name recognition. Many times, it's the area you are in.

The smaller the area being served, the more local firms tend to do business together. Larger areas, such as major cities, aren't as concerned with doing business locally but take note of the trend with your customers. Believe me, I've used the "I'm local" strategy many times, because many suburban and rural people want to know your great, great grandfathers came over on the Mayflower together with theirs or they won't trust you.

Exploring further, you may want to analyze why your firm lost sales or were not able to close certain deals. Again, generating reports of old prospects will help. If the prior salespeople recorded why they didn't close, the reason may expose who your competition is and what their strengths and weaknesses are.

Once you have conducted this type of analysis, you can then decide whether or not to target specific niches or a specific area. Once this is complete, you will then be able to generate a valuable lead list.

Generating Your Lead List

Once you have done your due diligence in identifying who your best audience will be, it's time to start generating leads.

The first types of leads you should identify and gather are those leads that your firm has prospected in the past. These are the leads that are not being worked on, no salesperson is assigned to or the prior salesperson is no longer with the company. These become your easiest leads to go after because a connection may have already been made. Your sales pitch for these candidates will be easier due to familiarity. It's not exactly a cold call – it's a warmer call.

After that, you can find a good lead list company to gather your new leads. Lists from lead list companies are the best way to go in my opinion. They allow you to zoom in on specific industries, company size, revenue, type of corporation and someone to contact at a management level – the kind of information you researched. These lead lists may cost a bit of money, and some companies are not willing to pay for them (which in my opinion is foolish considering the amount of time spent gathering this data without the list).

In addition, most of these lead lists can be imported into a sales management program like HubSpot or Salesforce. The time saved on generating these lead lists and importing them into your sales management program, rather than manually finding and entering each one, is huge! While the non-lead list person is gathering such information, you will already have months' worth of leads ready and be making appointments from these calls.

Nevertheless, if you can't get this type of list, you can find lead info from trade associations that list their members, such as a chamber of commerce directory. You can also Google businesses or go to websites like Manta Media.

Setting the Groundwork

You've done your research. You've identified your prospects and, hopefully, your boss was willing to spend the money on a lead list. You purchased your leads and then imported them into your Sales Management System. You have "gathered your materials." Now we need to prepare the groundwork – where your bricks will be placed. A little more prep work is needed before you can begin to lay the bricks.

Study Your Competition

Certainly, knowing your competition is important. If you really want to waste time, go into a Discovery Meeting or a Proposal thinking you have the best offer and get trashed by the prospect when they tell you your price is too high, your services are minimal, you don't offer anything different, etc. Knowing what you are up against helps you have effective responses at the ready when faced with objections.

Do some investigating and find the answers to these questions about your competition.

- What do they offer?
- What's the difference between what they offer and what you offer?
- How do they get their customers?
- Are they in a trade association?
- Do they have an exclusive program?
- What is their area of influence?
- Are they the most reputable in this area?

KNOWING WHAT YOU ARE UP AGAINST HELPS YOU HAVE EFFECTIVE RESPONSES AT THE READY WHEN FACED WITH OBJECTIONS.

I'd like to take a moment to explain why this is so important and I'm going to use an example that you may love or hate: the New England Patriots. Yes, I happen to be a born and bred Boston guy, so that's my team. If it makes you feel better, I did grow up watching the Patriots lose frequently and even when they made it to the Super Bowl, they lost twice. So, we deserved a few wins. Enough of that.

The winning Patriots of the last twenty or so years have been excellent at studying their competition and exploiting their weaknesses. If the opposing team cannot stop a running game well, the Patriots' play sequence is geared toward running. If they find one cornerback who is not a fast runner, then they will put the faster runner on wide receiver to oppose that cornerback. If the opposing coach is poor at time management, then the Patriots will try to stay on the field as much as possible. The Patriots have lived by the adage "you don't always have to win big; you just have to win." Exploiting weaknesses in their opponents is one way to do this.

Such is your sales game. You don't have to be the ultimate superstar salesperson to get a sale. You just have to know what to say to your prospect that will persuade them to buy from you. It's even better when you know your opponent so well that you can tailor your presentation to address objections you know will arise because of your competition.

You must study who and what you are up against to know how to exploit their weaknesses and accentuate your strengths. Keep in mind, they will also point out your company's or product's shortcomings as well. Without a proper defense, they will gouge a huge gaping hole in your chances.

Also important in knowing your competition is trying to learn their approach or sales style. What does your competitor stress as their primary attribute? Are they the best servicing company? Do they tout their number of years in business or that they are family owned? What does their proposal look like? A little digging on your end will go a long way. If you can identify *how* your competition will sell their product, you'll stand a good chance of moving the ball into the end zone.

The Other Local Thing

One other time-consuming mistake you can make is trying to pitch a business that is not local – that is, they are a store within a chain or part of a franchise. For example, if you go into a Home Depot to try to sell them insurance, they will most likely tell you to contact their corporate headquarters as that is where the insurance for all of their stores is handled. The same goes for Walmart or Pottery Barn or most chain stores.

There may also be companies you are not familiar with that also have corporate offices outside of your area or state. I've done this a few times. I've walked in and talked to a manager or other employee and they simply say, "We don't handle that here. It's handled out of our corporate office in Whatever, Whatever."

Some businesses, however, are franchised and may be franchised under a local, private name. For example, a single franchise owner of Kentucky Fried Chicken stores may have five or six restaurants but operate under the name Smith Restaurant Group. Many chain retail stores, restaurants and hotels/motels are run like that too.

Unless you have the money and resources to pursue out-of-state corporate-type prospects, it is best to identify those businesses you can reach locally through a franchise operation. Lead list companies usually have an option for you to choose businesses that are headquartered in the territory you are targeting.

Usually, in lead list generators, there is an option to filter businesses where the headquarters are located in the area you are targeting. If the headquarters are not located in your targeted territory, then you can choose to exclude them. If your boss won't buy you a lead list, however, then you should check the business's website first. It will save you an unnecessary, disappointing call or in-person visit. *Don't waste money on poor leads.*

Laying the Stones

Let's review all that we have discussed in this chapter and come up with a bullet list of the ways to identify your best prospect. Remember that in the previous chapter we identified your main objectives – you are always going after the most likely, highest valued prospect in the least amount of time.

- You first must have a product or service that is meaningful and meets a need.
- You've done your research, so you are more confident you can identify a potential audience.
- They have adequate representation in the area you are targeting (there are enough businesses to reach).
- They may not be the kind of prospects you are comfortable with, but your firm has had much success working with these types of businesses.
- They fit the demographic of your existing client base (size, number of employees, sales, structure, etc.).
- You have a competitive price.
- You are aware of who your competition is, including their strengths and weaknesses both in product and approach.
- The business has headquarters where you are targeting and is not run by an out-of-state corporate office (unless you can target this).

The whole objective here is for you to gather enough leads so that when you are ready to make your calls, you can simply "lay the bricks." In other words, you pick up the phone and start calling because your prep work has set you up to do that.

Reaching Out to Your Prospects

Being a Civil War enthusiast, I love to study the maps from various battles that took place. I like to see how one army decided where and how they were going to attack, where the areas of advantage were and how they would set up formations.

In similar fashion, you will want to examine your territory and decide how you will "invade." Whether or not you are actually assigned a territory or you are working in a vertical or niche market that crosses territories, when you start pounding the pavement, having a mapped-out strategy is a true time-saver.

I like to use the nuclear bomb approach. If you've ever seen the way a nuclear bomb explodes, you will see the initial detonation in one area, then you'll see a round cloud expanding from that initial area, spreading out further and further and eventually becoming thinner and thinner.

In the same way, I like to penetrate my territory by starting closest to my office (or home) and moving out in increments as I go along. Why? Because the people nearest to you are the ones most likely to buy from you. They are also, more likely to have heard of or know of your company.

Once you have saturated the core part of your territory and gained some customers, you can expand out of the core circle to the next ring and use the clients in your core area as a reference. Those customers will be closer to the next ring and new prospects may be familiar with them when giving references. You should still dedicate some time to the outer parts of your territory initially, so you have a head start when you eventually hit those parts more fervently.

Even in a niche line of attack, this strategy accomplishes the same goal.

I'll give you an example. When I was a territory salesperson, I worked in three counties. I knew the most people in the county I lived in, of course, and knew very few people in the other two counties. So, what I did was two-fold. I focused most of my time in the core county, but also made some efforts to get my name out in the other two counties. Eventually, I generated enough qualified prospects and new customers in my core county to begin putting more effort into the next ring. Then, I adjusted my time focusing more in the next ring while balancing time needed in the core ring. Finally, I got to the third ring.

As a side note, (in case you are wondering) I could not start my radius where the company was located because another salesperson was assigned to that territory.

Nevertheless, my full strategic map was basically three rings, circling where I lived. Ring one was the core territory (twenty-five-mile radius), rings two and three expanded to the other territories (ten-to-twenty-five miles each).

Zooming in a little further, you might have a large city with several businesses to target. This, again, is where a line of attack from a mapping standpoint will be invaluable. What sections of town will give you the most likely, highest valued opportunities in the shortest amount of time? What areas have a significant number of qualified leads?

You can't go wrong by mapping out a strategy, and you can even go so far as to map out a daily route. Especially with door-to-door cold calling you can map out where you will visit using GPS and addresses.

Mapping out your plan of attack coordinates your strategy more effectively and efficiently and also provides you with the ability to monitor success. When we get to Chapter 9, we will examine further how and why mapping fits in to the overall strategy.

5

IT'S ALL IN THE RATIOS

"It is the set of the sails, not the direction of the wind that determines which way we will go."

—JIM ROHN

erhaps you are afraid that you won't make it in the sales profession. Who isn't?

Seriously, if you truly are scared of your success as a salesperson, it's due to one reason – failure. You are afraid you won't make any sales, especially if you are a newbie. Believe me, I've been there too. I had no idea if it were even possible to get a sale when I started.

The problem is you are asking the wrong question and, in doing so, it puts you on the defensive. You become reactionary in your approach. You start waiting for it to come to you. You start hoping you'll get a break. You start avoiding the hard sales tactics like cold calling and door-to-door selling and revert to less effective and less personal methods like email or social media. Then, when nothing is happening, you say, "I'm just not cut out for sales."

Then, you take another type of job, like a Service Manager or IT Programmer, that you are not really interested in. You become bored and unsatisfied. Not that those are bad fields, but what if they are not for you? What if you are a good salesperson but just took the wrong approach? Maybe you had a defeatist mentality to start with?

So then, let's regroup before you become the next trash collector in your town.

The question is not, "Will I get a sale?" You have lost the battle already by asking that question. The pro-active, assertive and more-likely-to-succeed question is, "What will it take for me to get a sale?" Do you see the difference in the approach and attitude of these two questions already?

As long as you have a product or service that meets a need and provides value – or better yet is a legal requirement – then someone will buy from you. Believe me, I've seen salespeople that were charismatic, animated, well-groomed and attractive as well as salespeople who were boring, monotone and sloppy. Yet, all of them had one thing in common. They sold something to someone.

As a matter of fact, if you don't believe me, try this experiment. Where you are working now, go ask every salesperson in your organization who has had at least a year in sales, of any kind, whether or not they actually sold something at some time. It doesn't matter whether they sold something at your current workplace, or somewhere else. I can almost guarantee you that every one of them will have answered yes. Why? Because of what I am about to explain to you.

Sales Ratios - Measuring Your Success

Sales Ratios are essentially the measure of how much work it takes to finally close a sale.

Every salesperson out there has sales activity ratios. Some people just don't keep track of them. Not measuring and recording them is hazardous to your efforts. Without tracking your ratios, you will never know how and where to improve.

Sales Ratios measure the amount of specific activity it takes to get a sale. Depending on your process, each activity itself may have a ratio but, ultimately, the *Hit Ratio* is the end result and what you continuously want to improve.

The process itself looks like this. I'll use my own numbers as an example.

On average, it takes thirty contacts to get one appointment. Thus, my *Contact to Appointment Ratio* is 30:1

The *Decision-Maker to Appointment Ratio* is the number of decision-makers you actually reached who agreed to meet with you.

It takes three appointments to get a sale. That's a 3:1 *Proposal to Sale Ratio.*

My ultimate *Hit Ratio*, however is 90:3:1. It takes ninety contacts to get three appointments to get one sale.

Now, let's dissect these equations.

The Contact to Appointment Ratio

First, it will take thirty contacts to get one appointment. When I talk about making thirty contacts, there is only one way to do this – cold calls. However, cold calls can be made in two ways – picking up the phone and contacting a decision-maker or walking into the business.

I'm talking about calls where you're playing games with the gate-keeper and the contact is in a meeting, or on vacation or you get sent to voice mail. I'm talking about the contact who is too busy right at the moment and tells you to call back and then is not there on the day they told you to call. I'm talking about that walk-in where the store owner is busy with a customer or where the "No Soliciting" sign hangs on the window that you ignored and now reception is blasting you for it.

What I am not talking about here is a LinkedIn or Facebook message. I firmly believe that people who fear what they perceive as personal rejection rely on those methods to get sales – and they don't get many. Likewise, I'm not talking about an email blast to the "Valuable Shop Owner" or "Town Resident" either.

Granted, technically LinkedIn and email blasts are a form of "contact" but let's take a serious look at these various methods by evaluating each one's success ratio.

For example, suppose you send out 1,000 emails and receive three responses, providing you with a Contact to Appointment Ratio of 1,000:3. You follow up on those three and you ultimately propose to two and one actually makes a purchase. In that case, your Hit Ratio is 1,000:3:1.

Maybe LinkedIn messaging produces a 750:3:1 ratio.

In any event, it's important to start measuring these ratios as you will eventually learn what is the most effective way to reach your audience. Chances are that you will end up using more than one method or a combination of methods. Regardless, the question is still, "What will it take for me to get a sale?" Add to this, however, the cost to get a sale.

It's one thing to buy a lead list and start calling. That has a cost. There is also a travel cost to driving around, stopping door to door. Email blasts and social medial emails may also have a fee. Ultimately, your best approach will be to find the method that costs the least and brings the most.

The Decision-Maker to Appointment Ratio

This is really a sub-ratio within a ratio but nevertheless it's still important to examine.

The question we are answering here is, "How many decision-makers did I speak with to secure an appointment?" This is different from just, "How many calls did I make in general to secure an appointment?" The latter includes voice messages, follow ups, dealing with gatekeepers, etc.

While your general Contact to Appointment Ratio is 30:1, your Decision-Maker to Appointment Ratio is 10:1.

The Decision-Maker to Appointment Ratio comes from a philosophy of mine with regard to prospecting. "The best answer is an answer, even if it is a no."

I will not stop pursuing the decision-maker until I have been able to make my sales pitch and get an answer from that person. If it takes numerous calls and visits, I will get in touch with that person and get an answer. This is where you can make some excellent headway and actually gain a reputation as a great salesperson.

Many times, salespeople give up after one or two calls. They feel that they will never reach the person and, realistically, in some cases, you won't. Many times I've walked into a business where I have to ring a bell to get in or I must find the decision-maker's number and contact them on the foyer phone. These entrances are usually equipped with cameras too and the prospects can see who you are and may avoid you.

More often than not, however, persistence will get you to the person, even if you have to mug them in the parking lot. No, you won't need to mug them but I do know of salespeople who have waited in parking lots to try to reach prospects when they left their offices. In this day and age, you probably don't want to take that approach or you could be brought up on stalking charges or something similar.

To summarize and provide an example, if you made thirty calls and got one appointment, your Contact to Appointment Ratio is 30:1. If, within those thirty calls, you reached ten decision-makers and offered your pitch, your Contact to Decision-Maker to Appointment Ratio would be 30:10:1.

The Decision-Maker to Appointment ratio is good to know because, if nothing else, it helps you improve your methods to get to a decision-maker through analysis of your approach. It also gauges the effectiveness of your sales pitch or pitches.

The Proposal to Sales Ratio

The last phase of the Sales Ratio comes during this Proposal Stage – the appointment where you present your solution to your client's needs. Let's say that for every three appointments, you will get a sale. Since your Contact to Decision-Maker to Appointment Ratio is 30:10:1, that means you need to make ninety calls, speak to thirty decision-makers within those calls and secure three proposal appointments in order to get a sale.

You're probably thinking, "You just told us how to find and know our audience. Now you're telling us we may only get one sale out of three appointments?" If they are all pre-qualified, why wouldn't they all be sales?

That's a good and valid question. Here is where the human component comes in. Up to this point, you have made mostly technically based pre-qualification assumptions. You know it's the kind of business you can pursue but there may be some detail that was not considered during the initial sales pitch that disqualifies the business. More than that, however, it is very difficult to measure their commitment level without personally meeting with them.

IT IS VERY DIFFICULT TO MEASURE A PROSPECT'S COMMITMENT LEVEL WITHOUT PERSONALLY MEETING WITH THEM.

Let me tell you a story about my very first sales appointment. When I began selling insurance, in 1992, I sold homeowner's and auto insurance to local residents. My first call was to a woman and I still remember her name – but I'll call her Betty. "Hello M. Betty. This is Chris Carangelo from X Insurance. We can save you money on your homeowner's insurance and provide you with excellent coverage. Would you be willing to meet with me so I can get some information?"

Betty responds, "Yes! That would be awesome!"

I'm like, "That was easy! I was made for this! I'm going to be the next Larry Bird of Sales" (dating myself a little here). So, I go to Betty's house and meet with her. She agrees to give me all of her home and auto information and I complete my applications. I tell her I can get her a quote in a day or so and meet with her again to go over it. She said, "Yeah, that sounds good. I'll be happy to go with you."

Now, I'm thinking, "In ten years I'm going to be the CEO of a huge agency!"

Two days go by. I got my quotes and put together a nice proposal. I was ready to make my first sale. Dial, dial, dial – dial, dial, dial, dial (we didn't have cell phones yet). "Hello M. Betty. This is Chris Carangelo from X-Insurance and I was calling to see if I could meet with you and go over your homeowner's and auto quotes."

"Oh, sorry, Chris. I already put my coverage with Metropolitan Insurance. The guy was here yesterday."

Can you say sad trombone? Whah, whah, whah, whaaaaahhhhh.

"I thought you were going to let me give you a quote? And you seemed very interested."

Betty answered, "Yeah, he just got me the quote quicker and was cheaper than what I had so I went with him."

Why do I embarrass myself by telling you this story? Because the lesson learned here is that if a sale seems too easy, it probably won't end up a sale. That's one thing I learned. But the more important lesson was that I could have picked up cues or asked certain questions to determine her seriousness and commitment to buying from me. I'll get into this later in the book, but the point here is that you won't really be able to pre-qualify the personal aspects of your prospect until you meet with them. There are cases where, for one reason or another, there is little to no hope of a sale.

Furthermore, you might find that even if you get the information you need from a prospect and they seem interested, your company may not be able to offer a piece of something that will be the deal breaker. For example, your best insurance company to offer this product may not be able to write workers compensation insurance because of the claims history or they have operations in a state the company is not licensed in.

You may have gotten this far and your prospect is willing to review your proposal, however that doesn't mean you are guaranteed to get a sale. The prospect, in the end, just may not go with you. Again, we'll cover this aspect in detail later, but this is part of what makes up your overall ratio – your Hit Ratio.

The Hit Ratio

Finally, when you put all of the ratios together, you will come up with your Hit Ratio.

As I mentioned earlier, my Hit Ratio is 90:30:3:1. This means for every ninety contacts I make, I make my pitch to thirty decision-makers, from which I will secure three appointments to present my proposal, and that will ultimately end up in one sale – 90:30:3:1 or Contacts to Decision-Makers to Appointments to Sales.

The ultimate role of monitoring ratios is two-fold. First you want to measure the activities needed to get a sale as mentioned before. The other component, however, is time management. How will you fit these activities into your daily or weekly schedule. Prospecting takes a great deal of time, so once you start scheduling appointments, putting together proposals and conducting actual sales presentations, you will always need to make room for prospecting so that your pipeline will constantly be flowing.

Factors Affecting Your Ratios

When calculating your ratio, keep in mind that it will be an *average*. There will be times when you might make one hundred calls and get two appointments, for example. On the flip side, you might make five calls and get three appointments. It's not always the exact same formula. The ratios reflect averages.

In essence, the law of large numbers creates a guide for you so that you will be able to calculate how much time and effort will go into meeting or exceeding your goals.

Another important factor that will impact your ratio is the time of year – for your prospective clients and the world generally. During slow seasons or slow months, you will still need to keep your appointment levels up. Many times, the goals are still the same regardless of the month or season, and your pay comes from meeting those goals. Because you still need to get your three appointments, you may have to increase the number of contacts you make during that time. Fear not, however, because during the busier or more prosperous months, the number of contacts may decrease.

How to Improve Your Hit Ratios

When you begin your sales journey, you are embarking mostly on the unknown and the uncertain. The longer you continue, the easier it gets and the more confident you will become. A vital key to success is your continuous tracking and follow-up. If you are consistent and accurate in tracking and follow-up, it will inevitably improve your Sales Ratios. We will cover tracking your progress in more detail in Chapter 9, but for now we'll look at how deferred and recycled leads can enhance your Hit Ratio.

IF YOU ARE CONSISTENT AND ACCURATE IN TRACKING AND FOLLOW-UP, IT WILL INEVITABLY IMPROVE YOUR SALES RATIOS.

Deferred Leads

Let's say you start with a lead list of five hundred prospects. At first, you don't know much about these prospects in terms of timing or availability. So, you call Prospect X for example and X tells you they are not available right now but asks you to call back in two weeks.

This is a positive outcome because you can mark this person for a follow-up in two weeks and, when you call, you can now say that they told you to call back. The lead is warmer than the first cold call. In another case, the prospect might tell you to call back in another month because their contract comes up at that time. Again, this lead now becomes warmer.

Over time, these deferred leads begin to build up and your prospect list as a whole gets warmer. Thus, these follow-up leads (which still count as contacts in your formulas) are more likely to meet with you and perhaps buy from you.

Recycled Leads

Recycled leads are similar to deferred leads, but you have already proposed a product or service to them and they declined at the end. Depending on the reason, such as price, time or prior contract requirement, you may want to try selling to this prospect again at a future date.

It is very common in insurance sales, especially when targeting larger businesses, that a salesperson may propose several times before actually landing the final sale. This is a matter of judgment and experience, of course, as you don't want to practice quote every potential client. But there might be a future opportunity for some reason and that will also "heat up" your lead list.

Gaining Confidence or Facing Reality

Ratios, from an emotional standpoint, provide security and confidence. With ratios, you do not have to be concerned with whether or not you are a "good salesperson." A good salesperson conducts the right quantity of activities and makes good decisions to be successful. They measure the amount of work it takes to secure a sale.

The other great quality of monitoring and using ratios is you can match your numbers to those of your peers or competitors. By measuring your ratios against others, you will be able to determine whether your individual efforts need to improve, or whether the product or service as a whole is the right one to be selling. As I mentioned before, the better the product or service – that is, the more it meets a need or benefits your audience – the less effort it will take to sell.

So, in your analysis, if your Hit Ratio was 90:30:3:1 from past successes and now it's 150:20:3:1 – a significant difference – you will need to make some considerations. First, it would make sense to confide in your peers to see if their ratios are similar. Then, you can determine whether you need to improve individually, or if the product or service is not as desirable as you'd like.

The dose of reality comes when you conclude that the amount of work that goes into a sale is too great. You then realize there might be better products or services for you to put your efforts into. The hard part in this is that it takes time to reach this conclusion. You can't decide this in one week; it might take months and you now may have lost an opportunity.

On the other hand, your ratio might be much better than your peers or your industry as a whole, which means you've gained more knowledge and experience. Then, you will be able to write books and do infomercials. Best of all, however, you've been able to build your book of customers.

Don't Take It Personally

The eye roll, the sigh, the hang up, the abrupt no, the avoidance of you at a party or in a crowd. When the number of noes is greater than the number of yeses, which is common in sales, it can play with your self-esteem. Over time, you might think people just hate you and that can feel really bad.

Encouragement here might help. First of all, try to remember this. How could someone hate you when they just met you? In other words, is it really you, personally, or is it something else that's bothering them? Truth is, if sales is really more about the situation, and your objective is to be in the right place at the right time, then, most likely, you are in the wrong place at the wrong time. Your situation is not favorable at the moment.

Consider this example. You're doing a walk-in for a business. The decision-maker of that business is very busy. They've got meetings coming up. They've got a problem employee they'll have to fire. They've got customers demanding responses for their own services. Then, all of a sudden, you walk in.

Be realistic. Would you be happy if you were that busy and someone walked in to sell you something? Probably not.

You also have to remember that although you are offering a product or service that will bring value to your prospect, you are asking them to give you something. Conversely, if it were a customer of theirs, the customer is giving them something. Therefore, the prospect has to give up time to get something, so they can spend time giving you something.

You also have to keep in mind that you are not the only salesperson who approached them. In both the advertising and insurance fields that I worked in, I could tell you numerous times where the prospect's reaction was, "You are the tenth person who called me this month," or "I get so many calls about this." So that brings another frustration element to the equation.

If someone gets really nasty with you, however, you can respond with a kind question. "Excuse me, but don't you have to sell your product and service to stay in business? Would you like it if your salespeople were treated this way?" If anything, it brings that person back to reality in that they realize that you are just doing your job and that's the way business works. I've diffused a few situations just like that.

You can also simply address that you know the person is busy and you don't want to bother them at an inopportune time. Ask them if there is a better time for you to speak with them.

In any event, you have to remember that this is a game of numbers and ratios. Someone will see the value you are bringing to their business. Someone will eventually be kind and accept your offer. But always keep in mind that this is not about you as a person. It is about what you are doing and you are not doing anything wrong or bad by trying to sell your product. (Disclaimer: providing what you are selling is legal.)

6

PROSPECTING – WHAT'S YOUR OBJECTIVE?

"The trouble with not having a goal is that you can spend your life running up and down the field and never score."

—BILL COPELAND

Sales and Relationships

When they were growing up, I used to tell my two children that relationships are much like sales. Why? Because if a relationship is not going to work, it's better to find out in the dating stage, or as early as possible, before you end up at the other end, years later, married, with children and in a bitter divorce.

Please understand. I am not anti-marriage and I was not discouraging my children from getting into relationships. What I was doing was advising them to look for the qualities in their significant others that would contribute to a long-lasting, healthy relationship – and to accept what they found. If they found there were things about the other person that they believed would not work for them, or would jeopardize their relationship in the long run, then they had to make the hard decision to break it off. The sooner they did this, the better, because obviously they would have the opportunity to seek out other relationships that may work out better.

By settling for conditions you know are counter-productive or detrimental to your relationship, you will find yourself constantly trying to repair it or you will end up in eventual pain.

The same problem applies in sales (maybe not as painful, but similar nonetheless). Why go through the contact, the appointment, the gathering of information, the analysis of options, the generation of a proposal, the consultation from peers and the final presentation only to get a big fat no? Why waste time when you could be spending your time on more likely, higher valued opportunities?

Granted, there is no guarantee that you can filter out every positive and negative quality of your prospects, just like there is no guarantee you can comprehensively identify the pros and cons of a significant other. If you could do that, lawyers would be out of business and there would be no divorce. You're objective, then, is to try your best to weigh your prospect's commitment level in addition to your ability to meet their need.

Let's start at the point where you are going to contact your prospects. At this point, you have done your research. You found your audience. You know what your company is good at. You know who your competition is and what your strengths and weaknesses are. Now, it's time to get in touch with those on your lead lists.

Making Contact

I've trained several people, especially with door-to-door selling, and I found their answers funny when I asked them, "What do you hope to accomplish when we go in there?" Mind you, a trainer asked me this same question at one time and I got it wrong too.

Answers varied from, "I just want to leave them my card and have them call me," to "I'm going to let them know what we do," to "I'm going to tell them we can save them money."

The guy who trained me, laughed when I said, "I'm going to tell them who we are and what we do."

Right off the bat, he said, "That is not going to help you much." I was dumbfounded! They don't want help, I thought?

He then followed up with, "Your objective should be one thing. You just want to get an appointment. That's all you need to do." Wow! My pride just went down like a shrinking cartoon character playing the sad trombone. It didn't make sense to me because it seemed so simple. Nevertheless, the logic makes total sense to me now.

That day and that training session changed my sales life. What a simple concept! My entire approach changed after that as well. Even my sales pitch became geared toward that very objective – land the appointment.

> **MY SALES PITCH BECAME GEARED TOWARD THAT VERY OBJECTIVE – LAND THE APPOINTMENT.**

Just to clarify, let's look at the difference between the "sales only" approach versus the "get an appointment" approach. Here's the scenario: Salesperson X walks into a business and asks for the owner who happens to be there. M. Smith comes out to meet with you.

- **Sales Only:** Hello, M. Smith, I'm Salesperson X from Y Insurance Company. I wanted to let you know we are the premier company that offers the best coverage and can save you money on your insurance. I'm hoping you will keep us in mind when your insurance comes up for renewal. Here is my card. Please contact me when the renewal date for your insurance approaches.

- **Get an Appointment:** Hello M. Smith, I'm Salesperson X from Y Insurance Company. I understand you will be reviewing your insurance soon. I'm a local insurance agent here in town and would like to meet with you to analyze your current insurance program and see where we may identify any gaps in coverage. We may be able to provide better options and possibly lower your premiums. A meeting will help us gather the necessary information to make these determinations. Would you be available on Thursday at 10:00 a.m.?"

Do you see how these two approaches differ? The first approach is babbling. Salesperson X is probably saying what every other salesperson is saying anyway. There is no call to action, no prompting, no need for the prospect to react. It's a dead-end pitch.

The second approach, however, created urgency, provided a reason for the importance of a meeting and a call to action. The sales pitch was more about why the meeting was necessary than it was trying to explain why the company, product or service is so great.

Remember, you only have about 15-30 seconds to plead your case. You were given time by this prospect, but they don't have all day. You will annoy them if you go on too long. You will also hurt the efforts of others, or even yours in the future, if you abuse your chance. Make it quick, get to the point and ask for an appointment.

With the appointment approach, you are making it clear and giving respect by showing them you recognize their situation and want to work with them at a time that works better for them.

Once you get your foot in the door, you will eventually get to sell whatever you need to. You will be able to tell them exactly what they need to hear. A sit-down meeting will capture their attention more effectively and they can't just hang up on you or not respond. In addition, you can now make further connections to encourage a deeper commitment from your prospect.

Follow Up, Follow Up, Follow Up

Again, my key philosophy when it comes to prospecting is, "The best answer is a response, even if it is a no."

My goal in contacting prospects is to always, where practical, get to the decision-maker and persuade them to give me a yes or no answer. Even if their answer is an eventual no, and I can't get any subsequent appointment, I consider it a step closer to my next sale.

You may have to call, follow up, follow up, follow up, find them at a Chamber event, send them an email, message them on LinkedIn, etc. Whatever you do, don't give up until you get an answer from the decision-maker.

Think of it like this. Remember when you were in the dating stage and you were at that bar? You saw that very attractive person on the other side of the room. You wanted to approach them but you were nervous. Or, you immediately assumed they were too good for you or out of your league. But you really didn't know anything about that person and, worst of all, you would never really know if they were interested in you. Why? Simply because you didn't ask.

Let's take this a step further. Let's say you did go up and start talking to that person. After a while, things seemed to be going well so you ask them to go to dinner with you. They're busy on the night you requested. Do you drop it there? No, you try another night. Or, they may be traveling a lot and aren't available for a committed relationship. Maybe, for now, at least, you keep in contact and put any relationship prospects on the backburner. Or, you work around that person's schedule.

The point in all of this is that until you get an absolute yes or no answer, you will never know what the opportunity is and will never know if it was worth pursuing.

Follow up means keep trying until you get the absolute yes or no answer. Yes, you will have to play games with Robin the office assistant a few times. Yes, you will have to chase the prospect when they tell you to call them in two weeks, every two weeks. Yes, you might have to show up at the business. In the end, however, all you want from them is a yes or no decision. This is so important because many salespeople I've worked with call someone two or three times and then give up.

As I mentioned before, you do have to be realistic. Perhaps, after ten tries, if you are getting the same result, such as you will only reach Robin and they will put you to voice mail and that's all that will ever happen, then you should call it quits. Yes, there is a point where you cut your losses. But you can't give up too soon. Remember the concept of being in the right place at the right time. You increase your chances of this happening by initiating more contacts.

Have a Date and Time Ready

One of the most effective ways to secure the appointment is to name your date and time, specifically. Don't be vague or beat around the bush. You have Tuesday the 10th at 11:00 a.m. open. Suggest that date and time. Have two more backups as well. Leaving the date and time open creates work for the other person and, again, could be the reason they do not want to meet. You say, "I can visit you at your office Tuesday the 10th at 11:00 a.m. Will that work for you?" If it doesn't, offer the next date and time until you can land one.

You should also send an invitation through Outlook, or whatever email/calendar program you use. Send the invite. Don't worry if they accept it or not. Just send it. It's on their calendar now.

Never Call to Confirm

If you want me to write a paragraph or two to explain this, I will. Basically, if you call to confirm the appointment, most likely, the prospect will make an excuse to cancel. It happens way too many times, so why take the chance? If you show up, even if the candidate doesn't want to see you, they realize they made the commitment.

I Object!

I'll be honest. I froze many times when a prospect objected to my sales pitch, especially if they were abrupt about it or sounded angry. It put me at a loss for words. I just couldn't think of a response quickly enough to change the person's mind. I came to learn, however, I was not the only one who experienced this.

One day, I attended an insurance sales seminar where the instructor led us through one of the best exercises having to do with handling objections.

The instructor of this class, himself a seasoned salesperson, told us as follows. Over time, whatever your field and with whatever you are selling, you will begin to face the same general objections. Remember, when you are faced with an objection, it is not because of you, personally (unless your company or industry has a poor reputation). Most of the time, an objection comes from being in the wrong place at the wrong time or simply need. Consider the very common and frequently used objection, "I'm not interested." Why isn't the person interested in what you have to sell? Here are some possible reasons.

1. The person is too busy to talk to you at the moment and needs a quick way to get off the phone.
2. The person is overwhelmed with other responsibilities and sees your call as simply more work.
3. The person may have just transacted a similar deal.
4. You may be the tenth person calling about the same thing this week.
5. The person is quitting the job and doesn't care.

Okay, I put number five there because I wanted a list of five. It looks better. But it is a possibility, right?

The bottom line is you are making a request that this person give you time and consideration.

Responding to this person will take practice because maybe they are abrupt and/or very busy. These types of people also have a tendency to say they are not interested and simply hang up.

So, we developed a series of objection cards. This instructor determined that in the insurance industry there were thirty-five common objections to making the appointment to review a prospect's insurance. No more, no less. The idea was to list three things on each card: the actual objection, the reason behind the objection and the response to the objection that would help overcome it.

By listing these three components, we would be able to acknowledge the objection, understand the reason behind the objection and offer a sufficient response to overcome that objection.

A very tactful way to handle someone being abrupt is to acknowledge that you are taking up their time or realizing they are busy. You may even address the fact that they have had numerous salespeople call them. By acknowledging their frustration, you diffuse the situation and they see you are showing some empathy.

THE GOAL IN HANDLING OBJECTIONS IS TO CONTINUE OPENING THE DOORS THE PROSPECT IS CLOSING.

The goal in handling objections is to continue opening the doors the prospect is closing until the last door cannot be opened or you have gotten the result you came for. Remember, we are trying to bring the prospect to a final decision.

Let's try the exercise using the "I'm not interested" objection.

"M. Jones, hello, this is John Smith from the X Company. I was calling because we heard your company was on the cusp of releasing a new software product and we would like to help you create an advertising campaign that will reach the targeted audience you are looking for. I'd like to set up a time to meet with you so we can examine the prospects of success using our approach."

"I'm not interested."

"Can I just ask you one question?"

"Sure."

"Has anyone else tried to offer advertising to you?"

"Yes, I've received three other calls this week."

"M. Jones, I know you are busy and want to respect your time. I know who those companies might be and can assure you we are doing something very different. But I don't want to take up your time right now as it may take a little more than a phone call to discuss. Can we set up a time that is better for you? I have Wednesday the 15th at 2:00 p.m. open. Will that work for you?"

Again, there is no magic formula, but being prepared for objections is far more effective than simply freezing up. You can at least be ready and increase your chances for overcoming the objective and getting what you want. You also exude more confidence to the prospect and gain their respect by anticipating they will object in that way.

If you do receive a common objection like, "I've done this before and it didn't work well," perhaps you can build into your initial pitch a line that addresses this objection up front. "And I understand that some other firms have not had as much success as we have, but you may be interested in seeing how we've helped our customers succeed."

Think of it as preparing for a debate, like politicians do. The goal of debates is for the candidates to sell themselves and their positions to the public to secure votes. At least, that's how it's supposed to work. So, what do they do? They prepare for the debate. They anticipate which questions will be asked during the debate and prepare a convincing response. They also prepare for their opponent to counter their response. So, they develop another response or perhaps countering arguments to provide a solid overall case.

In a way, you are preparing for such a debate. You will present your case, and your prospect will counter your position. You need to respond back in such a way that you will persuade that prospect to accept your proposition. The good news is that selling a product is not as emotional or hostile as promoting a political position.

In a nutshell, you do not want to ever sell the store up front. Your goal should be to simply get to the first step. Then the next one. Then the next one.

Think of it like a football team. The chances of a team making one, giant play to get them all the way down the field to a touchdown are far less than smaller, more frequent plays that move the team incrementally until they reach the goal line. A "long bomb" play is certainly possible, but most likely it won't be enough to live on. The shorter incremental plays bring more success.

Your aim is to get enough yardage to keep you moving forward, until you reach the goal line.

THE DISCOVERY MEETING

"You got to know when to hold 'em, know when to fold 'em
Know when to walk away and know when to run
You never count your money when you're sittin' at the table
There'll be time enough for countin' when the dealin's done."

—KENNY ROGERS, "THE GAMBLER"

So, you got the appointment! You got your foot in the door. You will be meeting with the head honcho, the decision-maker. The game has started and you have the chance to play your hand to the best of your ability.

Friend, this is where you are more likely to make your sale. This is where you need to diagnose the prospect's needs *and* their given situation. You will need to analyze not only their technical, actual need, but you will also have to gauge their level of commitment – how serious are they about doing business with you?

From experience, I can tell you this. When the time comes for you to make a presentation and this particular candidate's eventual answer is a no, I guarantee that you will be able to go back to the Discovery Meeting and figure out the root cause of that declination.

The Discovery Meeting, much like your initial pitch, is also not the place for you to sell. I can see you're getting aggravated. You want to tell your potential buyer about all the wonderful things you and your company can do for them. Hold on! You will get to that.

Here is where patience and a little courage comes in. The goal of a Discovery Meeting is to learn as much as you can about your prospect and diagnose the likelihood that you will be able to offer them anything. You must also judge a little character here. Yes, in sales, we judge. If we don't, we'll end up broke. You have to use some street smarts to figure out if this prospect is serious about buying from you, are they using you to get a better price from the incumbent vendor or are they just afraid to say no.

Get to the Decision-Maker

First of all, make sure you are meeting with *the* decision-maker. If you are not, then learn about the relationship this person has with the decision-maker. Are they a manager? Are they the head of the department?

Also, you need to figure out how influential your interviewee is with the decision-maker. Some decision-makers are simply the owner, but they rely on certain managers to decide and merely ask for the blessing. Others will simply be the gatekeeper, taking all of your information, only to say later that "The owner decided we do not want to go in this direction."

YOU NEED TO GET TO THE DECISION-MAKER. PERIOD.

You need to get to the decision-maker. Period. If you can't get to the decision-maker in your Discovery Meeting, you should request that they be in the proposal presentation. If they cannot, or will not attend, then you should tell them you will not do the presentation until they can be present. Why? Because this is more often than not a tactic used to get rid of you. If the decision-maker will not be present to make a decision, then they have already made their decision. You will find, most of the time, that you won't get the business.

The bottom line is that the decision-maker was too cowardly to say no up front so they do something worse – waste your time. Believe me. I did a self-poll and found I was unsuccessful 99% of the time when I did not present my proposal to the decision-maker. This was conducted for fifty Discovery Meetings.

The Two Areas of Focus

Once you have secured an appointment with your prospect and you have conducted your interview, you will know whether or not there is a real opportunity here. Asking the right questions and being real with the potential buyer from the beginning can be the difference between meeting and exceeding goals or showing up on the lower end of the sales board. Your time is valuable and this is where the value of your time is determined.

When conducting a Discovery Meeting, your efforts to uncover this opportunity potential should focus on two main areas: the technical discovery and the prospect's level of commitment. Can you meet their needs and are they willing to buy from you? Let's take a look at each aspect.

The Technical Discovery

The technical discovery has to do with learning about the prospect's business and their overall buying situation. It uncovers the answers to such questions as:

- What do they offer?
- Who is their audience?
- How does their product or service benefit their clients?
- Do they have a real need for what you are offering?
- Are they a stabile business and are they growing?
- Do they have long-term or short-term needs?

The technical part of your discovery can uncover what this business is actually about and whether or not it is truly a business that has a need for and can benefit from what you have to offer. Much of your technical discovery can be accomplished beforehand by looking at such things as the client's website, Dun & Bradstreet reports, State Labor Department sites. There may be some details, however, that were not evident in your initial research that you may need to dig deeper into with the prospect during the meeting. The primary goal is to uncover their core needs so you will be able to respond with viable solutions.

What you don't want to do in this phase is ask basic questions, like their address and phone number or how many locations they run. You don't want to look lazy and unprepared. Look that information up beforehand.

As an example, if you are in advertising, you might learn that the prospect spends a considerable amount of money on magazine advertising. You might inquire as to why? They may tell you that they believe this magazine reaches their specific audience and they have procured a significant number of sales from those advertisements. When you analyze this claim (later on), you might find that the magazine only reaches a small group of people in a given area. Perhaps a search engine product you offer will be able to reach far more people who are actively asking for their product or service, but this prospect has no real way to "catch" them online other than a website. The point is you are looking for technical weaknesses and "openings." These will be specific to your industry. The more you know about your own product or service, the more likely you will be able to identify these vulnerabilities.

Eventually, you will come up with a general discovery strategy and a few technical questions. These will either open up another series of questions and, thus, opportunities, or they might give you the information you need to decide that you won't be able to meet some or all of their needs.

When I was doing advertising sales, I had three simple questions:

1. What do they offer?
2. Who is their audience and where are they located?
3. How are they reaching this audience now?

Those three questions almost always pointed me toward an opportunity. Because advertising is not an exact science, I could find ways to show our products and services would benefit them in a more substantial way.

Think of the technical aspect of your Discovery Meeting like a football coach. What does the football coach look for in their opposing team? They want to know what their overall play style is. Are they a running team? Do they pass more? Where do this team's strengths and weaknesses lie? Do they have a strong running defense? Are their cornerbacks slower than their wide receivers? What are the plays they commonly go with? Are they more zone defense or man-to-man?

You are essentially trying to figure out if there is an opening from the technical aspect and where it lies. The challenge is to get enough detail to figure this out. It will take practice and experience, but eventually, you will know how to zoom in on the deal-breaking opportunities. It also takes discipline in this area because usually a salesperson's tendency is to determine the prospect's personal commitment. So, without further ado, let's talk about the personal aspect of your discovery.

The Prospect's Level of Commitment

Have you ever played chess? The goal is to get the opponent in such a vulnerable position that they will have nowhere else to go, won't have any weapons or soldiers left to do battle and your next, and final, move forces them to concede.

Now, let's be clear here. We are not in battle with the prospect. We do not need to be demanding or hostile. We do not need to manipulate, bully or coerce this person. The reason for my chess analogy is to show that by your line of questioning, you will move the prospect to reveal their true intent in dealing with you. You will essentially, craftily be asking them, "Are you seriously thinking about buying from us or are you wasting our time?"

Again, each industry will be different and so will your line of questioning. But some of the answers you should look for – in all industries

– will help you determine your prospect's intentions and personal level of commitment.

- First, you want to uncover what is most important to your prospect. Price? Service? Discounts? The reputation of the companies/vendors they work with? Etc.

- Why were they interested in having this meeting? Are they just "looking"? Do they normally shop around? How frequently?

- What is their decision-making process? Will you be following up with a presentation? Will the decision-maker be present in this presentation? Is there a vote to decide?

- And then, the final question after all is said and done, should actually start with a summary.

  "So, M. Prospect, I just want to make sure I understand your situation. You are having trouble with service from your current vendor and cannot operate effectively with such uncertain delivery and response times. You told me that price and quality of this product is important to you. Is this correct? Is there anything else?"

Now, you will ask the last question, and this is probably the most important one. "M. Prospect, if we are able to provide evidence of our responsiveness and service standards, our competitive prices and that we provide the highest quality of products and services, will you be ready to give us your business and part with your current vendor?"

It may seem a bit forward to ask that question, but you have a right to know. Your time and money are as valuable as theirs and they must understand that wasting your time is inconsiderate. It's one thing to genuinely not know and they might just come out and say that, which is fine. You will just have to knock 'em dead with your presentation. But they may just confess that it will be really hard to part with their current vendor. They might be friends, relatives, part of the same club or group. The Mafia might have forced them to work with them, etc.

Whatever the reason is, if you don't think you will be able to overcome that relationship, you might just want to walk away.

Don't be ashamed to ask that question. You have a valid reason for it. Perhaps you've been burned in the past. And you can even say that to a prospect. "Listen, I ask the question because it takes a lot of time and effort to come up with my proposal and it involves several people. I just want to make sure we are not wasting each other's time."

By the end of your Discovery Meeting, you should be able to gauge your potential of succeeding with this client. I like to use a percentage, such as, "I have a 60% chance of closing this sale technically, but 80% personally." Doing it like this tells you where your focus needs to be.

If your technical chances are less, that's where you may need more work and vice-versa.

> You got to know when to hold 'em,
> know when to fold 'em
> Know when to walk away and
> know when to run

BY THE END OF YOUR DISCOVERY MEETING, YOU SHOULD BE ABLE TO GAUGE YOUR POTENTIAL OF SUCCEEDING WITH THIS CLIENT.

Tough to Walk Away; Worse to be Rejected

If you are new to sales and hungry, turning away business may sound like a crazy idea. Walk away? Do you know what I had to do to get this appointment? I can persuade these people! I just need to get my foot in the door and it's all over.

Think of this like dating. Would you rather find out early on if a relationship is going to work or not, or wait until marriage, kids and a divorce to find out it didn't? It's better to find out earlier.

The funny thing is that as you build up your pipeline, consistently meet or exceed your goals and you become more established and experienced, *you* will become pickier about who you want to do business with, rather than hoping your prospect will like you.

Generally speaking, walking away from a prospect is not an exact science. Using my likelihood of success mentioned above, I would determine ahead of time that anything less than 50% would not be worth the effort. Anything is possible, yes. The price buyer may have changed their mind and saw the real value of what you are offering. The frequent shopper got sick of always shopping and was willing to sign a long-term contract. Maybe the prospect's brother-in-law who was providing insurance just got caught in an affair and they're pissed. Anything is possible.

But what you are also trying to figure out is if you have another, better opportunity to spend time on. Will spending time on this prospect take you away from getting three more appointments and perhaps better opportunities? I can't give you the exact answer in your particular situation, of course, but this line of thinking will help you decide for yourself.

What if, you are in the slow part of your sales cycle and you have not secured as many appointments as you would have liked to? You have an appointment with a prospect and believe, after your Discovery Meeting, that there is a 50% chance of success. To secure another meeting will take more calls and time. You might get two more appointments in place of this one. You might have had real trouble this month, so maybe it's worth taking the risk.

For me, if it's 50% or more and I have the time, I'd take the chance. At least it's a known. You don't know what kind of prospects you haven't met with yet and whether or not they too might end up at 50%. The other key component is the decision-maker being present. If I'm presenting to a manager only, then fuhgeddaboudit! That manager is almost certainly going to say, "My boss said we are not interested."

If you conclude there is less than a 50% chance of success, then don't waste your time. All you will gain is another learning experience.

Is Your Prospect a Dud?

Again, there is no exact science or measuring tool that will accurately, with one-hundred-percent certainty conclude that your prospect will buy from you or not. There are some signs, however, that you should never ignore. These red flags should also be weighed heavily in your decision to go forward or walk away. Because you are reading *Life of a Salesperson* and hopefully either you or someone else bought it, I'll give you some of my tips from the experience files.

- **The Brush-Off.** The prospect tells you to email your proposal. UNNNGGHH! (That's the buzzer sounding.) That's the easiest way to avoid giving an answer or simply stating no and that's why they are asking for it this way. Plus, it shows that what you are offering is not important to them or they have not thought enough about it. If they can't sit with you and go over your proposal, then they do not care. *One small exception* to this rule is the product you are selling. If it's software or something small for which you don't need to give a presentation, or if it's a common practice to email quotes, then by all means proceed.

- **The Price-Comparison Shopper.** They gave you a quick, "come on in" and already have information ready. In fact, it's a well-organized pile of paper. This most likely means they are shopping for price and are looking for an "apples to apples" comparison. Depending on what you are offering, if they don't give you the opportunity to explain why your product or service is different or they won't sit down and discuss what they really want or value, then they have no wants or values other than price. If you really need a sale, great, but you have to be exceedingly lower. Furthermore, they will likely give their current vendor a last look and you will find yourself fighting for this business more frequently than you have time for.

- **The Family Member.** There is a relative involved. No matter how dumb, incompetent, lazy or useless cousin Earl is, he needs a job and it's up to family to support family. The son-in-law is married to the prospect's daughter and if he's not working for dad-in-law, then they are always asking for money anyway. Family ties are very hard to break. Unless a family is totally dysfunctional and hates each other, they are probably not going to trust you, who came out of nowhere. Family will stick to family.

- **The Shady Dealer.** They don't provide all of the information you need but tell you to put your "best foot forward." Think about how nonsensical that is. They want you to give your best options and price, but they won't give you what you needed to do it. It can't possibly be your best. The clear tactic here is as long as you are in the dark, then you will never know if your offering was better or worse and the prospect knows this. So, they can always turn around and say you were too expensive or you missed something that they needed, etc. If the prospect can't be open and honest with you, then they are not being open and honest, and most likely their intent is dubious.

- **The Sentinel.** You meet with a manager or some other "picket." In the American Civil War, a picket was a person who went ahead of the infantry to scan an area and determine the strength of the enemy. In this case, this person was told to meet with you simply to gather information because the decision-maker was too lazy to meet with you in person. Or to be fair, they get so many sales calls like this, they like to meet and push off just to be polite. Whatever the case may be, the manager is really a gatekeeper. They're just another level in the video game you'll have to conquer, once you get past Robin the office assistant.

Judging Your Prospect

Over time, you will start to see tactics or characteristics of prospects that provide indications of commitment seriousness. It might seem odd or counter-productive, but many times candidates will waste your time with no intent of buying and there are various reasons for this.

As an example, in insurance, one of the most common ways to figure out whether a prospect is serious about working with you or is just price shopping is *how* they provide information. If you contact them and they easily agree to meet with you, that's great. However, when you arrive, the person has a package of information all ready for you and hands you basically all of the necessary applications and other info. That, in and of itself, is not bad either, but they are not really willing to sit down and discuss the information they gave you, or they continuously say, "It's all there." Then you have a price shopper.

With regard to insurance, price shoppers will more often than not give their current agent a last look. This means after you take all of that time to input the information you received into your system, generate applications, send those applications to your insurance companies, negotiate coverage with the company, generate your proposal and meet with that prospect again to present your proposal, guess what? The prospect will take what you gave them, go to their current agent and say, "Can you beat this price?" The incumbent agent almost always says, "Why, yes! We can beat this price!" And voila! You just kept that prospect's premiums at bay.

Forget the fact that buyers never question the agent and say, "Well, if you got the premium down this year, why didn't you do that last year?" But that's another subject. The point is, the prospect was not at all serious about working with you.

> THE DISCOVERY MEETING IS WHERE INTELLIGENCE, STREET SMARTS, EXPERIENCE AND EMOTIONAL STRENGTH ALL COME TOGETHER.

Your Outcome

The Discovery Meeting, in my opinion, is truly the hardest part of the selling process. This is where intelligence, street smarts, experience and emotional strength all come together. You could be wrong, either way, about what you conclude or, you could be exactly right. Only time will tell, but the best thing you could do for yourself is be honest. The more honest you are, the less futile work you will likely have to do.

8

THE PROPOSAL

*"There is no power on earth that can neutralize
the influence of a high, simple and useful life."*

—BOOKER T. WASHINGTON

You gathered the information you needed. You interviewed your prospect. You are confident that from both a technical perspective and the personal commitment level, this prospect is a go. Now, it's time to develop your solution.

While Proposals for some products and services might be easier, the one focus every salesperson should keep their eye on is what that specific prospect told you was important to them. So, in developing your solution make sure that you will not only be able to meet those particular needs, but be clear in your presentation that you understood them and are addressing them.

The Same Ole, Same Ole

Let's face it. Our society is in a constant state of multi-tasking. Most people are in a hurry, have multiple meetings, have a heavy workload and a whole host of other things going on at home. Think of yourself having to sit down at a sales presentation with all that you have going on. How much would you like to hear about? What is the relevant information you need to make a decision?

The worst thing you can do is present a standard, canned Proposal that spends too much time on the history of your company, the backgrounds of the entire executive management team, all the facts and figures you would give to the IRS and the same bullet list of service standards you value that everyone else values.

Let me give you an example. In the insurance industry, you will most likely hear an insurance agent tout the following reasons a customer should do business with them.

- "We are a family-owned business" or "We are a 100th generation agency."
- "We have been providing insurance in the community since 19XX."
- "We represent multiple, reputable insurance carriers."
- "We provide excellent customer service."
- "We are part of this alliance or trade group."

What they should put in their Proposal to save time is, "We all say the same thing." In fact, I actually put together a brochure mocking this very thing. I listed the "Top Ten" insurance agent selling points. At the bottom of the brochure, I simply said, "We will find out what your needs are and find the best solutions to meet those needs." It still sounded a little cookie-cutter, but at least it wasn't what everyone else was saying.

Just think about this. Suppose the prospect is looking for another insurance option, and four agents offer Proposals. They all go through their bullet list of why the prospect should do business with them – all of the items noted above. Does this not diminish the power of each insurance agent when they all sound the same? They should just send one salesperson out for all four agents to save money!

Create Your Scenario

Many times you will be competing with another company for a prospect's business. On some occasions, you might be the only salesperson presenting a solution. It is very important that you keep the overall "presentation" scenario in mind. Let me give you a situation I commonly come across in my current position.

At this time, I am a Senior Marketing Representative for an insurance company. My job is to reach out to insurance agencies who have a contract with us. These agents are the salesforce and my job is to visit and encourage them to send their business our way. Most insurance agencies represent multiple insurance companies. These insurance companies also employ marketing representatives like me.

Let's say I visit a stronger producing agency once a month. Let's also assume that this agency represents ten other insurance companies, but perhaps they see the marketing staff from seven of them monthly as well.

That means eight people from different companies will visit the sales and service staff of this agency each month. All of them will try to do the same thing. They will try to persuade the agents to send business their way. Most marketing visits last about an hour. So, this agency must put aside eight hours a month to listen to marketing representatives and their schtick. When it's time for me to visit them, I don't know whether I am the first, the last or somewhere in the middle in terms of presenters. What I do know is that if I talk the whole time and spout off a plethora of information, they will retain very little of it. Why? Because eight of us marketing reps are visiting them once a month for an hour, so they might here eight hours of whatever.

Why do I bring this up? Because you must remember that you might not be the only person trying to sell your product or service. The potential buyer may have multiple vendors coming in to present as well. So, they may get bombarded with information.

What I learned from my role as a marketing rep is to focus in on the one or two things that a specific agent might need during my visit and *only* focus on those two things. And, in my presentation, I stress these two or three points over and over so they will retain the information I gave them. I try to add a little humor to the visits as well so they will remember me as a person. That's my personality.

YOU ARE NOT THE ONLY GAME IN TOWN AND YOU NEED TO MAKE YOUR PROPOSAL STAND OUT!

Nevertheless, the point is to be conscious of the possibility that you are not the only game in town and you need to make your Proposal stand out in a way that will be remembered.

The Potent Proposal

The main objective of your Proposal is to let the prospect know you heard what they said, you did your homework and you have provided a solution and/or a strategy that will help them be better off, or better than they were before. Believe it or not, if you follow this guideline, you will find that you will become more passionate and convincing with your presentation. It will show them that you didn't throw just another template together. You're not going to repeat canned sales pitches. The best part of this approach? You get to be you.

So, what is an effective way to develop your Proposal? First, identify your dealbreakers, your basics and your luxuries. Doing this helps you figure out where to spend your time during the presentation.

Another powerful part of your presentation starts with repeating and listing the items or concerns discussed in your Discovery Meeting. You can even start the page with "What you told us was important to you," or something to that effect.

This starts the chess game we spoke of in Chapter 7 and you are making the first move. By doing this, you are essentially setting the parameters of the discussion. This also puts you in control of the discussion by establishing the moves going forward. If the prospect throws in extra needs that were not discussed in the Discovery Meeting, you can then respond with, "Since this was not discussed in our prior meeting, we will have to look into this and get back to you." It saves you from having to look like a deer in the headlights and continues the process by committing to follow up.

Now, you have a roadmap to follow. You can now go through your Proposal and as you present, you can remind your prospect about items that were discussed as you offer your solutions.

I'd like to share a Proposal I gave one time for a railroad spike company. Their main concerns (gathered from our Discovery) was that a competitor from Brazil was getting far more orders than them throughout the United States. How was a foreign competitor gaining market share in this prospect's home turf? They were also trying to make their public aware of some of their other products, particularly marine-related spikes.

The problem is that there are very few railroad spike manufacturers in the world, so the competition is fierce. People go with what they know. As most of the advertisements were evident in trade magazines, that is where a great number of sales were attributed.

What I discovered in my follow-up research was that there was an entire audience, throughout the United States, that was actively searching on-line for railroad spikes. We are talking in the hundreds of thousands. I found the same result to a lesser degree for marine spikes.

I found the Brazilian competitor showed up on the first page of a Google search, while my prospect was somewhere on the second page. This was simply by default and perhaps not by any professional advertising effort.

My internal team and I came up with a couple of solutions that would cause my prospect to become the first result on the major search engine pages when certain terms were searched for. For all those people we found searching on-line for railroad and marine spikes, we would be able to show them that this prospect was the premier manufacturer.

Now, it came time for the Proposal presentation. My IT consultant and I sat down with the owner and the manager (I made sure I asked if the owner would be in the presentation first, by the way). Then, we went through my presentation. First, we identified the concerns and needs they shared with me in the Discovery Meeting. Then, we provided some numbers. I was able to discover the major trade magazines they advertised in. Then, we found out the circulation of those magazines. After that, I took those numbers and compared them to the overwhelming number of people we found that were searching on-line for their products.

Next, we showed that we could reach this specific audience in the US with ads and Search Engine Optimization. And we stressed that we were confident their competition was not doing any such advertising because of technical factors my IT consultant pointed out.

At the end of the Proposal, we provided enough evidence coupled with our solutions to prove that we would be able to reach a far greater domestic audience that was actively looking for their products while their competition was simply "showing up."

They had questions, of course. How would this work? What will the ads say? Etcetera. But once we were finished with the presentation, I pulled out my last stop – the closing that no one can argue with.

The Closing No One Can Argue With

Let me just say this. You cannot pull this off haphazardly and there is no magic trick to this closing. You are not faking anyone out and you are not presenting yourself as something you are not. If you are going to use the closing I am about to explain, you have to be able to back up what you say. You have to be sure you clearly understood what your prospect needed and what their specific situation entailed. You must have done enough research, you must have developed a solid solution, you must know what you are offering and how well it compares to your competition. You must also make sure you have addressed the dealbreakers. If you have done all this, you will be able to use your two most powerful weapons – truth and confidence.

Truth

A good salesperson with a sound product should not have to lie about anything. Sure, there is an art to embellishing certain things about your company or product. You also want to accentuate the positives of doing business with you and how your customers are wowed and all. At the end of the day, however, you will be able to base your solution and your sale on solid, truthful information and effort.

ESSENTIALLY, YOU HAVE OFFERED TRUTH AND WILL BE REWARDED WITH TRUST.

Your information, if questioned, can be verified and you are also able to overcome any objections regarding how your product and/or service will work because you learned about it inside and out. You have also created reasonable expectations that will last long into your relationship with this prospect after the sale. Essentially, you have offered truth and will be rewarded with trust.

Confidence

Listen, I'm not trying to land you a date here or help you become the most attractive person on the planet. That is not the confidence I am talking about here. This kind of confidence comes from knowing you worked hard, you listened to your prospect, made good decisions in developing your solution and believe in your ability to sell it.

People pick up on a con artist and they certainly will be able to deflate a poorly prepared presentation. But this is not going to be you because you did the work.

The Ask

I hate to burst your bubble here but this closing is no major secret or surprise. It's actually pretty obvious. But what it does is actually put your prospect in check mate. Obviously, you need to put this in your own words, but your closing should sound like this.

"M. Prospect, we reviewed with you the major concerns/needs that you had and listed them here. We conducted extensive research and collaborated with our team to come up with the solutions we are offering. What we presented here has addressed your concerns and needs and we have presented a sound strategy with positive, but realistic expectations. We know from past experience that these solutions will bring the successful results you desire. All we need now is for you to give us the go-ahead and we will be able to execute this right away. Can we proceed?"

The next step sounds very simple, but it's hard to do. That is, be quiet. Let this prospect think for a minute or two. Your silence will astound them. You are not hard selling! You are showing even more confidence *and* competence. Let them think. The secret here is you are thinking too. You are watching their reaction, their body language and reviewing what you presented to make sure you didn't miss anything.

Just be quiet and wait for their response. Don't get anxious either because their response will only be one of four things.

1. "Yes, we would like to proceed."
2. "What about?" Or, "We have some questions."
3. "We will need time to think about it."
4. "We really can't do this right now."

Translated, the four answers above are:

1. Yes.
2. Yes, after you answer our questions.
3. No, but we don't want to tell you to your face.
4. No, we were not open and honest with you.

What is so great about this closing? Number one, you are basically stating what you did. You explained your process. You also presented your end of the implied deal. The implied deal was that they told you what their concerns/needs were and you responded to those concerns and needs with a sound solution *with the assumption* that if you did so, they would accept your proposal and do business with you.

The last part of the closing is key, though, because you *have* to ask for the business. A boss of mine used to say this almost every day. "You don't ask, you don't get." In fact, even the Bible, in the Book of James, tells people that when they pray to God, "You have not, because you ask not." Even if they say no, they were going to say no anyway if you didn't ask, so you increase your chances by asking. The ask is an absolute must.

I have used that closing over and over and many more times than not, it worked. Clients saw that I cared, I was competent and, most of all, they knew I listened to them. It made me stand out because of one thing – responsiveness. I listened and responded. I was also not boring.

> THE LAST PART OF THE CLOSING IS KEY, THOUGH, BECAUSE YOU *HAVE* TO ASK FOR THE BUSINESS.

The Flip Side Is Good Too

The flip side to this is that, at the end of the day, your prospect could possibly still say no. It could happen and it probably will at times. As much as this moment might suck terribly, you should be extremely encouraged by it and here's why.

First, what your prospect can't do is argue with your closing. You did what you were supposed to do, so the problem does not lie with you, it lies with them. Second, they were not up front and possibly less than honest in laying out their situation or in giving you all of the information you needed. In the next chapter, we will go through monitoring your process. You will find different clues in your Discovery Meeting and Proposal that lead you to the root cause of your loss.

Just like in the cold calling process, you will learn more and more which prospects will have certain reservations. What you have learned from this process is how to pre-qualify your presentations better.

A Note About Team Presentations

A team presentation can be extremely effective or tremendously detrimental. There is no in between. It all depends on who is in the meeting with you. Some crucial key tips I will offer you from experience are these.

First, be sure to plan out and discuss the roles and goals of each participant on your team. You will explain A, B, C. Your manager will go over D, E and F. Your IT people will answer questions, etc. It is extremely important for everyone to "play their position." You will also need to allot time and be sure everyone understands who is in the meeting and how much time they have.

The last thing you want is for your pushy manager to start dominating the conversation talking about their six dogs and how much they like Scentsy® candles. Or that consultant who ends up talking about issues that were discussed in other meetings and time is ticking away. The bottom line is this: before any team presentation, discuss the prospect, the situation and the strategy you are going to execute.

The second thing you want to do is quickly ask who are the prospect's participants in your meeting and what are their roles. The reason for this is so that you can tailor your presentation, if necessary, to that audience. If there is an accounting person in the meeting, you may need to delve into numbers more. Or, if there is an HR person, you may need to address the benefits to employees. In any event, you simply want to make sure you are discussing relevant issues with appropriate people.

Finally, dress for the occasion. Don't wear a suit if the office is business casual. Some companies require professional attire but seriously, the only people who wear suits anymore are the people you can't trust: politicians, bankers and lawyers, etc. Your attire creates the atmosphere.

9

CONSTANTLY MONITOR YOUR PROGRESS

"When any real progress is made, we unlearned and learn anew what we thought we knew before."

—HENRY DAVID THOREAU

Think of every sale process like you would a competitive sport. You train, you condition, you study, you do whatever you need to do to become the best at your sport. The same idea applies in sales.

Review the Tapes

Not only should you be constantly studying, but you should also be learning from your experiences. In addition, not only are you the player but, in many ways, you are your own coach. And what do coaches do? They review the tapes.

You can't get better at anything if you are not willing to be honest with yourself. And you won't get better if you don't analyze your own process and progress.

In the insurance industry, we calculate probabilities by a concept known as the "law of large numbers." What this means is that the larger a sample base of people, property, businesses, etc., the more likely it is to predict the frequency and severity of a loss or a claim. This is how actuaries can figure out how many homeowners in suburban Boston will have fires, for example. Based on these numbers, they can better predict the premium to charge everyone in that area for homeowner's insurance because they know more accurately how to predict the probability of house fires.

YOU WON'T GET BETTER IF YOU DON'T ANALYZE YOUR OWN PROCESS AND PROGRESS.

The law of large numbers can also be applied to your sales experience because you will gather more and more data to develop your probabilities. It will help you to monitor your progress using the Sales Ratios as a guideline. The remainder of this chapter provides an outline of this process.

Assess Your Ratios

The first part of your monitoring is to calculate your own Sales Ratios (see Chapter 5).

- Contact to Appointment Ratio
  - Phone Calls
  - Walk-Ins
  - Email
  - Other
- Decision-Maker to Appointment Ratio
- Proposal to Sale Ratio
- Hit Ratio

How many contacts did you make to get an appointment on average? Break it down further if you can and determine how many appointments you secured by contact type. How many phone calls? How many walk-ins? How many emails, etc.

Next, focus on appointments. How many appointments did you get? Then, of course, how many appointments turned into presentations? Finally, how many presentations turned into sales?

The Lead Selection Stage

Once your ratios are calculated, you can begin to dive into the detail, starting with your call tracking reports. These are some of the questions to ask.

- How many calls did you make? Do you see a trend in number of calls for each lead?
- Was there a similar setup (such as an office assistant you had to clear, or did many of them have "No Soliciting" signs on their doors)?
- What was the makeup of the businesses that said yes? How big were they? Where were they located?
- Did you get to the decision-maker, or mostly managers?
- Why did they say no? Was there a common objection?

What you are looking for here are the quality of your leads and how you can improve them going forward. In your list of, say, one-thousand plumbers in your fifty-mile radius, what was the eventual number of calls, number of appointments and so on.

At the end of this analysis, you should be able to answer the questions below.

- Can I find more of the quality leads I've had success with?
- Have I saturated this market?

- Do we have a competitive product/service for this market?
- Was the effort worth the result on this market?

Your Pitch

As the saying goes, "Insanity is doing the same thing over and over again and expecting different results." Your pitch was supposed to be as short as possible, to the point and focused on getting an appointment.

- How did you formulate your opening line?
- Was it a strong introduction?
- Was your pitch too long?
- Did you compel your prospect to do anything?
- Did you get the same objection frequently?
- What was your Decision-Maker to Appointment Ratio using this pitch?
- What was the "connection" you used?

A note about your pitch here. You may want to track your success with a pitch more frequently. Give it the college try but if you find you're not getting anywhere after two hundred calls, for example, you may want to re-examine your pitch.

You want to ask if your pitch was the same to everyone or did you modify your pitch to different business types or businesses in a given location?

Most of all, what were the common objections you received? Were they just not interested? Did they not have time? Were you catching them at the wrong time of year? Was cousin Bob doing the same work for them?

Whatever the objections were, this will prepare you for the future. Based on those objections, you can either build something into your initial pitch or respond effectively with a follow-up question or point.

Analyze Your Discovery Meetings

I can't stress this enough. The Discovery Meeting is the root cause of a sale or a refusal. If you were diligent in your interview and information gathering and keen on the interviewee's responses, you will be able to figure out where the probability of your success was determined.

A thorough analysis of your Discovery Meetings should look at both the sales you closed and the ones you didn't. You may find a pattern in your chain of questioning or even the answers given that will lead you to clues. These clues will give you an idea of where you did well or need to improve.

Perhaps you did not do enough research ahead of time and, thus, your line of questioning didn't get to some real issues. Perhaps you were not direct enough with the prospect in determining their level of commitment. Let's admit it, sometimes people are jerks, so questions become confrontational to them and they get offended. But you and your time matters as much as theirs does.

The Technical Angle

This part is fairly easy to analyze. If you did not land the sale and you ask why they declined your offer, if it's a technical reason, they will simply identify it. This will point you to the obvious. Was it price? Was it a coverage? Was it some service aspect they felt they needed that you couldn't offer? Again, the technical part is easier to analyze and, over time, you will gather patterns of data that you can offer to management in efforts to improve.

Their Level of Commitment

Do you know what makes this part difficult? Living in denial. Seriously. Did you instinctively recognize red flags in your Discovery Meeting but choose to look beyond them? Be honest. We've

UNFORTUNATELY, LIVING IN THIS DENIAL IS SIMPLY REPEATING THE SAME MISTAKES.

all done it. It's human nature. Unfortunately, living in this denial is simply repeating the same mistakes.

Did you meet with the decision-maker? Did you ask where they were in their buying cycle? Did you ask what they liked about their current vendor? Did you ask why they were considering a different product or service? Did you ask if they would buy from you if you met their stated needs?

Also, try to judge the person you met.

- Was this person dismissive?

- Were they hurried?

- Did they have information ready for you?

- Did they cancel and reschedule multiple times?

Yes, judge the person you met. Because that person eventually said no to you and you don't want to get duped again. But also, be honest with yourself and how you asked the questions or approached the meeting.

Your Solution and Proposal

This part can be difficult because there may be many variables and angles you needed to consider when coming up with your final solution. Nevertheless, there are two main components you want to analyze: whether or not your solution actually met their needs and how you addressed those areas you were not able to provide solutions for.

The key here is to look at whether you truthfully understood what they needed and wanted and whether you showed concern for the fact that you couldn't meet a particular need or desire. What you don't want to do is state in your presentation that you can't provide something, but act like it wasn't important. That turns a prospect away. You want to make sure you knew you couldn't meet a need or desire and even ask if that creates a real problem. Again, showing concern is key.

Another question you want to ask yourself is whether or not you presented your case strongly enough. Did you do the proper research?

Were you able to show data and facts that properly built your case? Did you feel confident in what you were presenting?

Let's add some controversy to this. Did your manager or your executive team make you add some inane extra or condition that the company requires across the board? Did you have to use canned phrases or disclaimers? Was the manager in the presentation with you? I can honestly say, I fly better solo, but if I have to present as a team, I am very picky about who I want in the meetings with me.

I'm sure anyone reading this book can attest to the dilemma of a manager or some kind of expert joining you in a presentation and saying something so asinine, you just want to throw your hands in the air, walk out of the room and yell, "Next!" It's good to review this aspect because as much as you don't want to blame, there are other people on your team that can cost you a sale if they are not informed enough about the prospect or the situation. They may also be prone to say stupid things just to be heard.

Track Your Tracking

Take a good look at how you are tracking your activity.

- Do your notes reflect what was discussed in calls, a takeaway, a date for follow up and a follow-up activity?
- Did you miss follow-ups frequently?
- Were you able to get to all of your follow-ups in a given time?

What this may point out is that you are either not conducting enough activity or perhaps too much. The worst thing you can do is miss a highly likely opportunity simply because of oversight.

Also, examine your activity structure to make sure it follows a logical path. One activity leads to another and you are recording each step. Perhaps you could make more calls to find prospects, or less. In other words, if you are attempting to get an appointment, how many calls is it taking for you to do that? Are more calls required for a certain type or size of business? Does this occur because of the pitch you are using?

Another good reason to monitor tracking is because you want to find out the ratios of success with each type of contact. For example, how many phone calls is it taking to get an appointment? How many emails? How many walk-ins? This will also fine-tune your strategy when you learn your most effective contact method and can then figure out how many of each you will need to conduct each week or month.

Ask Others About Their Progress

It's not such a bad thing to find out how other salespeople are doing in your organization. Good salespeople learn from each other. Granted, you shouldn't give away certain information such as what you are working on specifically if you can avoid it (see Chapter 10).

You can, however, find out if other salespeople are finding prospects receptive to them and find out what feedback they are getting. You may find certain common responses that will provide indications as to your strengths and weaknesses, both individually and as a company.

GOOD SALESPEOPLE LEARN FROM EACH OTHER.

Identify New Opportunities or Niches

This can apply especially if you are assigned a territory as opposed to a vertical. If you are tackling a territory, chances are you are considered a generalist. Over time, however, you will begin to see what types of businesses you are having more success with.

Perhaps after securing contracts with two or three day-care centers, for example, you might uncover some real needs that you can meet for these businesses that you didn't know about. This can open a door to a whole new possible opportunity.

10

"OMERTÀ" AND OTHER TIPS

"Mad? I'm not mad at you. I'm proud of you. You took your first pinch like a man and you learned the two biggest things in life: Never rat on your friends and always keep your mouth shut."

—ROBERT DENIRO, *GOODFELLAS*

Omertà

also have a side-hobby. I love to study American History. I've studied the American Civil War for twelve years among other stages or eras. Lately, I've found an interest in organized crime that arose throughout the last two centuries. In my studies, I learned of a concept that the Mafia held dear to its success. It was called *"omertà."* Omertà is the art of keeping quiet and laying low. Successful gangsters were able to lay low and keep the release of information to the public at an absolute minimum. Then, there were guys like John Gotti, who loved the limelight and, consequently, attracted attention to themselves – the reason for their downfall.

What does this have to do with sales? Well, you know how I can tell a successful salesperson from a schmuck? The best salespeople employ *omertà*. They don't go around bragging to everyone about who they are in contact with and what they are doing. They keep that information to themselves unless they absolutely have to divulge information. They don't throw out names or dollar values to show they are a big shot.

As much as people you work with are your teammates, they are also your competitors. Unless there are strict, territorial or vertical boundaries, many times they will be going after what you are going after. They are also subject to goals just as you are. In a world where there is plenty of market share to go around, this isn't a problem. In most scenarios, however, you are selling a product or service that is being sold, has been sold, sold at one time to the prospects you will sell to or someone's heard of it.

You should only report your progress to your managers or other people who will offer support.

The other reason you should keep quiet is the chance that you might not get the sale. If you're out there bragging about a new Hollywood producer you're wining and dining so you can sell them insurance and they eventually turn you down, you will lose credibility and status. You will end up a "Yeah, sure" guy. Yeah, sure you got that big manufacturer's business. Yeah, sure you sold a car to the Governor.

At this point, I'm sure you get what I'm saying.

Track Your Progress Diligently and Thoroughly

Tracking progress is a tough part for many salespeople. Why? Because salespeople are, for the most part, people driven. Usually, their personalities are not of the type to record detail, let alone track their own whereabouts. It's just not in our nature. Of course, that's not everyone, but I'd bet for the most part, your DISC profile fell somewhere between the D and the I. You are the direct one, the one who is aggressive and you want it done and you want it now. You are the inspirational one, the one who is expressive, the one who likes to create and influence. Tracking details is boring.

I have to tell everyone what I'm doing, all the time? To some extent, the answer is yes as far as your company policy or management requires activity reporting. This, however, is mostly for your benefit. Tracking your activity and progress creates a greater likelihood that you will not miss an opportunity.

One day, I was attending a weekly sales meeting. The company I was working for used Salesforce as their primary Customer Management Tool. The director of sales posed the question, "Who is using Salesforce on a regular basis to track your activities?" Sure enough, the top salespeople raised their hands. It was evident that tracking activity is another crucial, albeit *boring,* part of our job.

TRACKING YOUR ACTIVITY AND PROGRESS CREATES A GREATER LIKELIHOOD THAT YOU WILL NOT MISS AN OPPORTUNITY.

Let me dig into a specific process – cold calling. Your notes would look something like the record below.

- *First Call* – Called Emily Jones. Office assistant said she was out of the office. Will return at 2:00 p.m.
- *Second Call* – Called Emily again. She said she would be willing to speak with me if I would call her on Friday at 10:00 a.m.
- *Third Call* – Spoke to Emily. She said she'd be willing to meet with me, but in April, two months before their contract renews.
- *Fourth Call* – Contacted Emily. She was away on a trip and will return Monday.
- *Fifth Call* – Spoke to Emily. Set up a meeting for Wednesday at 11:00 a.m.

It may seem basic here, but magnify this by thirty to one-hundred-and-fifty weekly calls. Are you going to remember when to follow up with each specific person and what to say to them when you call? It will be very difficult. Imagine, in the example above, if I missed recording the fourth call. I just forgot to. That call was my tip-off to call and set up the meeting I'd been trying to get for months. All the calls before that meant nothing if I didn't have a trail of calls, discussions and takeaways. Has this happened to you?

There are huge benefits of tracking your activity. For example, let's suppose you make a call and the office assistant informs you that your decision-maker has run out to get a sandwich for lunch. This might be a lead-in on the next call. "Hey John, this is Chris from X Company. Heard you got lunch. Any good places around you?"

John answers, "Yeah, I usually go to Paul's Cold Cuts down the street."

Now, you can say (if there is truth to it), "Oh, I know Paul's father, John. We grew up together."

John might answer, "Great people." In any event, you struck up a conversation that makes a connection and tears down the sales wall. At the very least, you can now proceed to your pitch with a more friendly prospect.

Keeping track of details like that will, first of all, provide you with a "To Do" list. It will also give you some additional intel about your prospect before or after you have a conversation.

The "To Do" list is invaluable. Here's another example. Let's say you are in the middle of a given month and you are a few thousand dollars short of your monthly goal. As you bring up your activity tracking, your upcoming activities might look like this for the week.

- Company A – Fourth Call – Try to set up meeting. Their contract comes up on June 12.

- Company B – Second Call – Bill is returning from X Conference.

- Company C – First Call – Janice belongs to Springfield Chamber of Commerce.

- Company D – Second Call – Sent brochure to Sandy G. Follow up to set up meeting.

- Company E – Fifth Call – Try to set up meeting with Bruce. Contract comes up in July. Mention PIAA golf outing he was in.

Do you see the importance of this level of tracking? You have three possible chances to set up three meetings here. If you need one more sale, this will likely get you there, if you just follow your schedule of recorded activities.

Tracking detailed activity is also beneficial during the process. You might pick up on details that will help you conduct a more thorough Discovery Meeting. You might need to remember some detail for your presentation. Whatever the case may be, it's meant to fill in gaps and help you remember. I was a Salesforce and HubSpot power user. I don't say this to brag, however. I say this because I have ADHD and need to stay organized as well as remember things that, without tracking, I would forget.

As far as your activity detail, you should try to record information that primarily gets you to the next step. At the very least, you want to record the data listed below.

- Where you are in the process.

- Who you spoke to.

- What was the result?

- When, if any, is your follow-up date and what is the action that needs to be taken?

Goals Will Change

Did you ever notice the more sales you make, the higher your employer will set your sales goals? Let's talk about punishing achievement! Many employers will increase your sales goals which inevitably pushes you even harder because now you have existing sales to retain and maintain, in addition to generating new sales.

Truthfully, in my view, I believe the reason for this action in many companies

> THE MORE SALES YOU MAKE, THE HIGHER YOUR EMPLOYER WILL SET YOUR SALES GOALS.

is that management understands that a salesperson will saturate their territory and once that happens, they will not expect significant growth after a few years. The salesperson then runs out of opportunities and unless they are transferred to another territory or niche, they will most likely resign and find employment elsewhere. Yes, this is a cold, hard reality.

Diversify, Diversify, Diversify

In a way, sales is like investing. You are investing your time and effort into something that is uncertain and hoping for a return. Like investing, almost every financial advisor would tell you to diversify your portfolio. Invest in multiple stocks, for example, because if one does poorly, another one will make up for it. Perhaps buying stocks and bonds together performs the same defensive strategy. The same idea should apply to sales.

I despise the idea of being a "generalist" and, yet, that is what I hear in the insurance industry all the time. A generalist, to me, is a person who waits and hopes for opportunity, has no real goal or direction and wastes huge amounts of time.

Granted, working as a territory salesperson positions you more as a generalist because it is area oriented, but that doesn't mean you should be contacting every business in the territory if you can't provide any benefit to 20% of those businesses.

You want immediate results (most likely, highest valued opportunities in the shortest amount of time). Try starting with three to five business types and track your progress. As one succeeds, you can focus more effort. As one appears not successful, you can switch to another business. At the end of the day, you become more of an expert in those areas of focus. You also create more realistic and direct goals and become more efficient trying to meet them.

One thing to keep in mind, however, is that it takes time. You can't make one hundred calls to fuel oil dealers, get one sale and think that this will not be profitable. Diversification takes into account that it takes time to develop each sector or business type you are targeting. Once you invest in a certain target, you should feel confident that you've done your due diligence on the overall opportunity (like an investor does). Part of your due diligence should include the steps outlined below.

- Research the number of opportunities and the likelihood of success.
- Project the volume you believe you will secure.
- Analyze your competition's strengths and weaknesses.
- Build your product and service knowledge as well as key differentiators.
- Estimate how quickly or slowly you will saturate this market.

On the other end, if you are considering abandoning a certain target in your portfolio, you will want to consider the following factors.

- Are there no opportunities left?
- Have your efforts exposed your product or service weaknesses that may not be overcome?
- Was your initial sales pitch effective and have you tried various approaches?
- Were you able to recognize in your Discovery Meetings the signs of low-level commitments?
- How many leads have you pursued in how much time?

Sometimes, your target strategy may just need adjustments. Other times, you may have discovered an obstacle you did not anticipate when you started and, thus, you can decide whether it is something you can overcome. If not, and the obstacle will take too much time and effort to correct, then you will be able to drop it and perhaps try another target.

In any event, diversification, as a part of the science of sales, is a way to become more effective by consolidating efforts.

Dress Code

There was a time when professional America instituted a dress code. Professional people wore suits. They were usually standard blue, gray, black or brown. They also wore ties. There was even a time when some salespeople actually had to wear hats. Dress hats, of course, not a Dallas Cowboys hat. (Is that considered a professional team? Just kidding.) Women also had certain dresses or outfits that were either acceptable or considered "unprofessional."

Enter the "Casual Work Environment." You can either blame them or be thankful for them, but the IT people of Silicon Valley started casual dress in the late 80s. In the 90s, we started to see "Casual Fridays." In the 2000s it became more of a daily thing.

Basically, casual dress is still nice, presentable clothing, but it's not uncomfortable, stuffy professional suits or dresses. Today, there are companies that allow jeans as long as you are not visiting customers.

I'm a big fan of casual dress for a few reasons. First of all, when I was starting out in my career, I was expected to dress like the suit-wearing CEO of the company. The problem was, I, like many others at my level, didn't make the CEO's salary and suits were not cheap. Back in the days of suits, whenever you got a new job, you had to weigh in the cost of clothing to what the company was offering you for a salary.

Secondly, why the heck did we have to wear suits to sit at a desk, in an office on the 15th floor when we only saw customers once in a while? I can see why the IT people wanted business casual, because they rarely saw customers. Nevertheless, a suit and tie is hot and uncomfortable and I'm sure many women would say the same about some of the outfits they had to wear. I work better when I feel more comfortable and I'm sure many other people feel similarly.

Third, you might actually turn off, or even scare off, your prospects. Let me tell you a little story. When I was selling advertising, part of my territory was Amish Country in central Pennsylvania. When I started, my company required us to wear suits every day. Well, one of my favorite suits was a black pinstripe suit which fit me very well and made me look, well, like a stereotypical Italian. I used to do walk-ins and many times, I'd walk in to Amish-owned businesses.

One day, I walked into an Amish-owned landscaping business and I started talking to the owner. The owner kept looking at me with this terrified look and I was like, "What's going on with this guy?" As I walked closer to him, he kept backing up. Literally! He was backing off as if I were going to shoot him or something. So, I walked away thinking the guy was a bit paranoid. Then, it happened again with another business. Then again!

I kept scratching my head thinking these people are just not used to seeing people from the outside world. Then it dawned on me, when I got home. I looked at my appearance. I examined what I was wearing. Sure enough, I looked like a Mafia hit man. I also noticed that I live in and work in rural America and these people are not used to city slicker-looking businesspeople. Granted, I'm sure there were other people who wore suits, but to be honest, central Pennsylvania did not have a large population of Italian Americans.

Saturating Your Territory or Niche

It happens. You've exhausted all of your leads. You've been able to identify and pursue the real opportunities. You've had your successes and your setbacks. You have very few opportunities left. You basically saturated your territory or your niche. What do you do next? Do you stay at the company and transfer to another territory or vertical? Do you shoot for a promotion since you performed so well?

While there are many considerations for your specific situation, the key point here is to recognize at the beginning of your journey with any employer that this is a likelihood. You have to plan your sales career for short-term and long-term goals. You don't want to be surprised at the end and find yourself out of a job for lack of sales.

TIME TO PUT IT INTO PRACTICE

Your Company's Sales Culture

hether you decide to work for an employer or you wish to start your own business, you want to make sure you are walking into a situation that will help you win. An employer is also a prospect in that you are selling yourself to them as much as they are selling themselves to you. Examine the product or service they are selling. Is it something that meets a need? Is it something different or new? What does the audience look like? And so on.

You also want to see what resources the employer has. Do they have a CRM, like Salesforce or HubSpot? Will they be willing to purchase leads? What are the goals and, of course, most importantly, how will you be paid? Also, try to meet with some of the sales staff during the interview process. Do they seem like real go-getters or are they more experienced and, having built a client base, they don't need to be that hungry anymore? Are the goals realistic?

The bottom line is you need to fit with your employer as much as your product or service needs to fit with your prospective audience.

Now Get Out There and Do It!

It's time for you to now go out there and put all that you learned into practice. I do too. Quite frankly, I can't keep writing more things because I have to get out and sell this book. So, I'm going to join you and put my game face on too.

As I said at the beginning of *Life of a Salesperson*, there is no get rich quick strategy to succeed in sales. Sales is both a science and an art which means you control how it gocs.

Carrying out a coordinated, well-thought-out strategy is the way to assure better success. And you control that strategy.

Be encouraged, as well. You are just as capable of succeeding in sales as anyone else is. Other people did it and were successful. What makes you any different?

The primary component is *you*. If you do the work, if you keep a strong sense of determination, if you exercise patience, if you understand the science of sales and how it works, you will be on a far better path than most of your competition

So, get out there, do the work and make money as if your life depended on it. Well, because it kind of does.

ACKNOWLEDGMENTS

Charles R. "Bud" Aronis (Died 2008)

Mr. Aronis, as I first called him (we were very professional then), saw the potential in this young Italian-American kid who was coming out of the construction trades and looking for a job. Bud hired me as a Personal Lines Customer Service Representative and trained me in the basics of insurance. From there, my career in insurance began. Thank you for taking the chance on me. Here I am over 30 years later.

Ellen Goldstein

Ellen was my Sales and Marketing Supervisor and was the person I wrote about who said, "You don't ask, you don't get." Ellen taught me persistence. She also is a cancer survivor and I watched her not only press on coaching me on getting new business, but making it through her own battles at the same time. Thanks to her, I realized that everything sales comes in seasons.

Roy Daugherty

Roy is a sales animal and the guy I would entrust the nuclear button to. Roy and I became a potent sales team in the digital and print advertising workspace. We cut some freakin' big deals and conquered central Pennsylvania's advertising market share. Roy has a plethora of knowledge, wisdom and skill and I was glad to have the opportunity to learn from him. He was also a great friend when I really needed one.

Steve Augello

Steve and I walked the streets looking for business. He is a real nuts-and-bolts salesperson and I learned a lot watching him fearlessly go into businesses even when they had "No Soliciting" signs. Heck, it was fun messing with the gatekeepers. Anyway, I also learned the art of sales and what to say in certain tough situations from watching Steve.

ABOUT THE AUTHOR

Chris-Michael Carangelo, CIC, ARM, CRIS, AU, has worked as a sales and marketing professional for over thirty years within two industries: insurance and advertising. Chris-Michael has enjoyed a strong track record of consistently meeting and exceeding goals and building a strong client base over the years. He is also considered an IT Power User and has served on numerous mentoring and marketing strategy initiatives.

Contact Chris-Michael about books, consultations or speaking to your group at chrismichaelcarangelo.com.

Made in the USA
Middletown, DE
28 October 2023

41370157R00071